Towards the Fullness of Christ

Towards the Fullness of Christ

Pastoral Care and Christian Maturity

MICHAEL JACOBS

'. . . *fully mature with the fullness of Christ*'
Ephesians 4:13

Darton, Longman and Todd
London

First published in 1988 by
Darton, Longman and Todd Ltd
89 Lillie Road, London SW6 1UD

British Library Cataloguing in Publication Data

Jacobs, Michael, *1941–*
Towards the fullness of Christ.
1. Christian church. Pastoral work.
Psychological aspects
I. Title
253.5

ISBN 0–232–51717–7

Phototypeset by Input Typesetting Ltd, London
Printed and bound in Great Britain by
Anchor Brendon Ltd, Tiptree, Essex

To Valerie,
companion in our
maturing years

Contents

Preface

The language used of human development applies to some extent to the writing of books. Ideas are conceived; they grow as a writer thinks them through; they both form the writer and are formed by him or her; they are matured through interaction with other people; and as they are written down they take on new shapes, until that moment comes when the last words are written. A new book is born, and rapidly has to be let go by the author to find its own way in the world. I am not the first to recognize the parallels between the experience of writing and the experience of being a parent.

Yet my earlier books were consciously matured over a long period of time before they were written down, and were tried and tested in teaching and discussion. This one has felt different. To be sure, it arises out of a short course I taught on Psychoanalysis and Religion, but it was not until a few months ago that the first serious writing began. In that time I have experienced different aspects of the subject coming together in a satisfying way; as well as thoughts and reading from long ago impinging upon my consciousness. The subject matter drove me as much as I tried to order it. It is as if the maturing (as I hope it is) of this study has taken place unconsciously over more than twenty-five years, and become part of my own search for integration. The result is a book which has felt smoother in its production than I could have expected, without the struggle that writing can sometimes be.

Whether or not the ideas are mature enough to stand the test of critical appraisal only the reader will tell. There is a danger that I have tried to create synthesis where none exists, even though I have been aware that such a synthesis is far from straightforward. Parallels exist, but not in any neat way.

I suspect that the chapters that follow only just begin to scratch the surface of a fascinating area of what is known these days as the 'interface' between psychology and religion. I hope my own and other people's ideas have been clearly enough set out for the reader to take the quest for integration further, without giving the impression that this particular synthesis is the last word. My closing paragraphs spell out the dangers of assuming that anything (at least in this field) is final.

I have also been aware that economic pressures on publishers force a writer to be briefer than he or she might otherwise prefer. This has necessitated my having to curb the desire for an extra paragraph here, or even a further chapter there, in order to fit the limit of pages which I recognize had to be set. I hope to have later opportunities of developing some of those tantalizing areas (such as guilt) in greater depth. The combined circumstances, of pressure of space and the urgency of the ideas pressing themselves upon me, mean inevitably that as much has gone unsaid as has been set down in these pages. While I make no claim to have written a definitive text, I hope that this attempt to draw together the psychology of human development generally, with the psychology of faith and moral development in particular, will open the reader's mind to the possibilities of the interdisciplinary dialogue that surely must take place more and more if pastoral care, and indeed the whole mission of the Church, is to take advantage of the various current ways of understanding persons. I have been careful to reference this short work as fully as possible, so that students of the subject can pursue for themselves these alternative paths to greater knowledge of the whole person.

At various stages of planning I have had those conversations with various colleagues which sharpen thinking and expand a writer's horizons, forcing him or her to clarify even further the ideas that are taking shape. Tony Chesterman, Kenneth Cracknell, Eric Forshaw, Isobel Hunter-Brown and Susan Parsons provided useful foils at the earliest stages, while Janet Watson and Moira Walker furnished me with new material or images which helped particular sections. My particular gratitude is extended to Derek Wright, who is not only an expert on Kohlberg (whose work I draw upon) and knew him personally, but who has been following a similar quest for integration to my own. I have had the benefit of some extensive discussions with him, and his early comments on chapter 2 were invaluable, providing confidence to develop the models in the succeeding chapters. Needless to say, these friends are not responsible either for the particular form which the book takes, nor for any errors which become apparent; but their help in its formation has made the task of writing an even greater pleasure.

Tugby, Leicestershire
December 1987

MICHAEL JACOBS

1

Aims

Fragmentation

Because of the many demands of day-to-day living, it is often difficult to take a long-term view of the direction in which life as a whole is moving. For those whose waking hours are filled with pressures of work and family, time seldom permits reflection on the future; although those who are unemployed, or who are compelled to live alone, may sometimes have too much time to dwell upon such matters, without the opportunity to act upon their thoughts. In the pastoral ministry too, long-term aims can be submerged by the daily round of administration and requests for help. Even if the question is asked, 'What is the overall aim of my ministry?', it is far from simple to answer, except through those commonly used generalizations such as 'bringing people to Jesus', 'building Christ's Church' or 'serving the needs of people', which spring readily, but somewhat loosely, to mind. In pastoral work, with its many facets, it is the short-term objectives that are the most obvious and pressing.

Pastoral care and counselling tends to be preoccupied with crises and problems. The sacramental ministry admittedly involves a slightly wider range of events, including occasions of celebration as well as times of sorrow and despair. Administrative tasks, of which there are many, often aim at keeping the ship moving and afloat, but seldom allow time to chart new directions. Pastoral ministry tends to concentrate upon segments of people's lives and experience, with little occasion to look at the directions of life as a whole, whether individual or corporate.

Such an immediate and rather fragmented ministry is probably inevitable, given the diversity of calls upon the pastor's time and energy. Indeed, it is perhaps the variety that comes with pastoral ministry which attracts men and women to engage with different people and their concerns. Such a ministry already implicitly deals with people as they develop and mature, and therefore forms a basis for the material in these chapters. Yet it is not so much the obvious stages of life, such as birth, adolescence, marriage or death, that form the subject of these chapters. Even though I refer to different ages, and developmental tasks that arise within them, my aim is rather to take a different perspective and to use different psychological theories to support and clarify ideas about personal development and the movement towards Christian maturity. Each new encounter in pastoral care provides a pastor with the chance of helping people to develop and grow as whole persons, although the wise pastor acknowledges that such a meeting may only move a particular person just a little further towards a fulfilling life. Even if most of us only change slowly, that should not prevent us from looking in greater depth at what the fullness of Christ might mean, since a more complete picture provides a clearer view of the destination that we claim lies behind all pastoral work. With a sense of direction, even the most mundane piece of pastoral care may provide an opportunity to help a person move one more step along their way.

'Fullness', 'wholeness' and 'maturity' are large concepts, which I have aimed to look at in more detail, although I do not presume to have arrived at a complete or definitive set of conclusions. If the reader is led to reflect upon wholeness, and yet arrives at different conclusions, I shall be just as content. My task is indeed an immense one, because a Christian view of maturity necessitates looking at the completeness, or fullness, of the whole person. By 'whole person' I mean a man or woman 'as an individual as well as part of a family and social unit . . . body, mind and spirit . . . with . . . psychological, ethical and theological frames of reference'.[1] This definition first appeared in the context of pastoral psychotherapy, but it is equally relevant to pastoral ministry. The themes in this book, therefore, attempt to follow the pathway to maturity and wholeness, dealing with the individual as an individual, in relationship to others, and to the community.

My concern is more with mind and spirit than with the body, although I do not forget that the body is an essential part of the whole person. The three different frames of reference – psychological, ethical and theological – I take to be equally important, so that in these chapters I concentrate upon the way in which faith and moral development are linked with personality, or what is often called 'psycho-social', development. The means of tackling such a huge task within the compass of a few pages, is to look at some of the major life themes, which to some extent coincide with different psychological stages in development. I provide an overview of these stages and themes in the next chapter, to show how they might relate to each other. I develop the themes in more detail in the rest of the book.

I am aware, of course, that the passage from which the title 'Fullness of Christ' is taken refers to the growing maturity of the whole Church, and not to the individual person. Elsewhere the calling of the individual is to 'be shaped to the likeness of his [God's] Son',[2] which makes me less uneasy about appropriating the fullness of Christ as a title for my theme. Moreover, the definition of the whole person cited in the last paragraph recognizes the individual as part of a family and social unit. Despite my emphasis on promoting the maturity of individual persons, I underline later that the maturity of an individual is marked by a deep sense of being part of the whole. Given the New Testament recognition that each individual is a member of the Body, and indeed the frequent interchangeability in the Old Testament of the One (the individual) and the Many (the tribe or the nation), it is of course equally possible to approach maturity and wholeness from another point of view, that of the development of society and community.

Such alternative perspectives of wholeness, either through the development of individuals or through working at the level of the group or society, are reflected in the division between developmental psychology (which concentrates upon the individual, in relation to others) and social psychology (which concentrates upon the group and the parts that individuals play within it). While these two approaches must clearly be held together, it is difficult to deal with both at once. Here I focus more on furthering the maturity of individuals ('the Kingdom of God is within you'[3]) than I do on the development of the Kingdom in society as a whole. This should not be taken as an indication of the lack of importance to me of this other aspect of the fullness of Christ. It is simply a reflection of my own background as first and foremost a pastoral counsellor, more used to dealing with individuals than with sociological or political issues.

It is also a reflection on the even more difficult task of enabling whole communities to move towards maturity. Two of the authors I draw upon have attempted to broaden their individual approach to look at the congregation as a whole. As I point out later, Fowler[4] hints that most congregations find it difficult to contain those who begin to move into more individualistic approaches to faith, and that few individualists are able to tolerate conventional congregations. Such an analysis, which I perceive as an accurate one, illustrates the much greater difficulty of helping a congregation to grow in maturity. Capps[5] makes a bold attempt to extend the pastor's care of the individual's life cycle to that of being a 'ritual co-ordinator' of the church life as a whole, and looks at healthy and unhealthy church communities. I return to his suggestions later, but they do not provide more than sketchy possibilities for the development of congregations as a whole.

Like Fowler and Capps, therefore, I base my own thinking on individual psychology. However, despite my own background of counselling, my interest here is far broader. I am concerned to address the area of general pastoral care, recognizing that a pastor has more extensive opportunities than a counsellor does to promote and encourage personal development.

Personal development proceeds on a number of fronts at once, and it is impossible in a short book to give adequate attention to the complexity of psycho-social development. I choose, for instance, to concentrate in later chapters upon faith issues more than upon interpersonal relationships or life stages as such, although I point out the way in which these are often linked. That being the case, it is worth taking this early opportunity of looking at the background of pastoral care as a whole, which provides opportunities for the growth and development of individuals through different life stages. Pastoral care helps people develop as whole persons, through crisis work, through rites of passage, and through educational programmes. These are all situations in which the particular concerns of the later chapters may often find expression, since developments of faith, of a sense of meaning and of moral thinking are both influenced by, and also influence attitudes to, life events.

Growth through Crisis

The idea of growth and development is important both in pastoral counselling, and in crisis intervention in pastoral care. In working with persons in distress, pastor and counsellor would like to do more than help people recover their equilibrium. Some crises enable people to develop in ways they could not have imagined possible when disaster first struck. Breakdown can lead to breakthrough. 'First-aid' pastoral care may be called for in the first instance, but it is sometimes possible to move beyond the immediate problems which the person brings to the pastor or counsellor; and the process of recovery can itself bring with it fresh insights and new learning about self and others.

The following serves as a brief example of the growth that is possible out of crisis work: a pastor is asked to call on members of a family who have lost a child in a road accident. The immediate circumstances compel the minister to concentrate upon the different feelings and thoughts which are out in the open. Such a tragic loss probably gives rise to shock, despair, and anger. More deeply buried feelings like guilt might emerge. Pastoral care may involve helping the parents and siblings to handle their memories of their lost child or their dashed hopes for the future. There is more than enough here for the pastor to attend to, and mourning may take a considerable time. Yet it is also possible that such a family tragedy leads parents and siblings beyond the death of the child, to the relationships within the family, to new ways in which the parents support each other, to more alertness to their other children's development. Pastoral care may provide an opportunity for helping the family members, each in their own way, to discover new aspects about their faith, about their God, or about the way they view life and death. If the family wishes for extended help in their distress, the pastor then may have a chance to work with them on these equally important areas, to help them look at wider issues, including the way in which their experience of death has changed their attitudes to living. The expressions of faith (or absence of it) will be different in each member of the family, partly depending upon their age, partly depending upon the emotional impact of the bereavement, and partly depending upon their respective levels of personal development.

It would be foolish, of course, to pretend that every call for pastoral care provides such opportunities. In pastoral work, as in pastoral counselling, it is sometimes the restoration of the status quo (life getting back to normal, as if little had happened) that is being asked for. People want to get rid of negative feelings rather than positively wishing to develop more mature ones. Furthermore, such an extension of pastoral care or counselling into matters of faith and meaning is only appropriate either when it is explicitly asked for or is sufficiently close to the surface for an implicit request for further help in that area to be clarified. Pastoral care and counselling should not be used to shepherd people into beliefs and attitudes which they are not asking for. Nevertheless, there are times when problems and difficulties bring with them opportunities for people to learn from experience, and to move beyond the presenting issues towards more satisfying and mature attitudes and relationships. My aim in introducing some of the current thinking about the development towards maturity, and particularly maturity of faith, is that it might be of value in more specialized pastoral care and counselling, as a person begins to move out of the immediate crisis, and starts to consider the implications of past experience for the present and the future.

Today's pastor may to some extent have become inhibited by the otherwise invaluable assistance which psychopathological understanding and counselling skills have provided for the enrichment of ministry. Psychology is generally much better at describing what can go wrong in human development than it is at advocating what might be right for it. It is often easier to understand how problems have arisen in the individual, than it is to predict what measures might prevent such problems. Perhaps also there is more fascination for deviations from the norm than there is for the ordinary, and more readiness to discuss pathology than normality. Healing is more interesting, more tangible, and perhaps more immediately rewarding, than the encouragement of a concept as intangible as wholeness. It is in fact difficult to agree a definition of normality, even though there are countless voices telling us what is wrong with people.

If the pastor is able to employ both counselling skills and knowledge of psychopathology sensitively, this aspect of ministry may appear to yield more obvious results than less immediately exciting duties. The ninety and nine can be left to their own devices in favour of the more appreciative rewards of supporting the one who is lost. In this book I dwell little on the pathological; my concern is much more with healthy development.

A further drawback to the ministry of pastoral counselling or of focused pastoral care is that it tends to limit the developmental opportunities to individuals in crisis, to those who are drawn to the pastor's attention because of their needs, or to those who request the 'services' of the Church. This may be because they are the type of people who are willing to share their difficulties, or because the distress they feel has become too much for them to cope with, and they are compelled by their inner turmoil to seek help. Regrettably this tends to mean that all the value that has come in the wake of the new interest in pastoral counselling is channelled in the direction of those who seek the pastor's help, but does not reach the majority who for one reason or another are reluctant to talk about their inner selves. Some are afraid of showing 'weakness' or of asking for help; others live lives where few deep problems present themselves, even if living is for them somewhat ordinary, with little incentive for movement and growth. How does the pastor bring the insights, and indeed the riches of the more personal work in which he or she is involved, to a wider audience, and to all those other people amongst whom the minister moves?

Growth through Life Changes

It is not easy to separate 'crisis' from life changes, because the end of one stage, and the start of the next, is often precipitated by or accompanied by some sort of crisis. Yet crisis need not be confined to negative experiences. Other life changes occur which are still turning points, even though they often present themselves more positively as full of hope and opportunity. Wesley Carr has drawn particular attention to the value of the occasional offices in pastoral care.[6] Pastoral ministry involves helping on many such occasions: for example, by preparing people for marriage and celebrating their public profession of their commitment to each other; baptism and confirmation are other examples of more obviously positive celebrations of life changes. To some extent pastoral care in these life changes provides a golden opportunity to look at relationships, at faith and at future decisions. They also appear to provide some churches with the excuse to push a theological line, even in some cases (I believe mistakenly) demanding expression of the right kind of faith, by which they appear to mean going to church, before agreeing to perform the ceremony. Such clergy would not ask the same requirements of a person in a crisis and, for example, refuse a funeral because the deceased failed to attend church.

In fact the people who ask for the Church's services at such positive times are expressing a type of faith, which they might find difficult to put into words. It may be a rather magical idea of religion, which we may fail to recognize as a legitimate stage of their faith development. They certainly look forward to the future and ask for it (and their marriage or child) to be blessed. There is so much more that pastoral care can do in these circumstances than push forms of religion which are inappropriate and unintelligible to those who request religious rites.

The pastoral situation can be used more relevantly to explore the potential for growth and development implicit in the wish for a rite to take them into the next stage of life. Baptism, confirmation and marriage preparation, sensitively conducted, can be an occasion for looking at the transition, and at the developments that are possible at a time of change. In marriage preparation this might include enabling a couple to look at their relationship, at their individuality as well as their togetherness, at their relationship to their parents and each other's families, at their ways of handling conflict, at decision-making, at the development of their sexual relationship, and at their ideas about having and bringing up children. It might include, in baptism and confirmation, chances to discuss relationships in families, the anxieties as well as the joys attendant upon the responsibilities of parenthood. Such subjects may be much more relevant than teaching sugar-coated sacramental theology. Such opportunities can make a major contribution to the way people think about personal and interpersonal growth and development, and may help couples and families to learn about the changes that take place in relationships as each person develops. It is by starting where people are, with the human factors of which they are most immediately aware, and by developing those, that people will catch glimpses of the more complex, largely invisible, theological relationships that lie at the heart of the religious tradition. Pastors need not become substitutes for Dr Spock or pose as amateur psychologists, but they need to understand the connections between human relationships and perceptions of the transcendent and be ready, as Jesus himself was, to use apparently mundane relationships between members of a family as relevant pointers to the Kingdom of Heaven.

It is worth stressing that in these circumstances pastoral care has to take account of what is especially relevant to a particular couple, or family. It is not necessarily helpful to look too widely at all the issues that might arise, or to talk too much in terms of the future. Since emotions (and anxieties too) also run high at times of more positive life changes, a couple or a family may find it impossible to acknowledge to themselves, let alone to the pastor, the less idealistic side of marriage or of becoming parents. Their preoccupation with the more immediate wedding or domestic plans will probably make it difficult for them to look very far ahead, and may make it hard for them to tune in to any talk about the religious aspects of the rite of passage. So while marriage or baptism preparation is of value in helping a couple to talk with each other about a limited number of issues, even illustrating aspects of faith from the human situation may do little more than sow seeds for later understanding.

Thus both crisis intervention in pastoral care (and here I would include bereavement), as well as the pastoral ministry to the more celebratory life transitions of birth, adolescence and marriage, provide opportunities to enable people to grow towards maturity, often as much in personal and interpersonal terms as in their faith. Yet pastoral care in both sets of circumstances is limited by the 'blinkers' that are almost inevitable in a specific situation or at a particular stage of life. At such times the focus of concern may have to be narrower than we might wish. Personal crisis or celebration of life's changes may not be the best time to try to help people develop in their faith beliefs or their moral attitudes, despite attempts on the part of some clergy to 'convert' people while they have them captive. The agenda is for the most part clear, set by those who are asking the Church for counsel, support or blessing.

While it is possible for such crises and life changes to be points of growth, the great advantage of the pastoral ministry is that it is available at times other than crisis points and rites of passage. A pastor is able to be alongside people at all points of their personal growth and their developing faith. Death, mortality, the dynamics in the family, or intimate relationships – to take some of the issues in the pastoral situations mentioned above – are with us all the time, even if it sometimes takes a calamity or a special occasion for us to recognize their significance. How often does pastoral ministry take other opportunities to address these issues, outside the more obvious points of crisis and change, and at times when people might be less anxious and more ready to reflect upon them?

I do not mean to appear critical of pastors and the pastoral ministry. The general practitioner too is nearly always so preoccupied with caring for the immediate, and in helping cure or alleviate illness and disease, that promotion of health and of more healthy ways of living has to be confined to a quick word of advice at the end of a short consultation, or left to the Health Education Council. Much of the frustration that is experienced by the caring professions is due to the fact that their time is taken up with an 'ambulance' or 'first-aid' work, so that they have no time, or even power, to tackle the circumstances that give rise to problems in the first place. The preventative, prophylactic, educative functions of the helper are squeezed out by the urgency and number of demands on her or his time. There are, however, opportunities in pastoral ministry, which other caring professions might well envy, to nurture growth and development in the ordinary routines of daily life.

Growth through Education

A particular advantage of pastoral ministry is that it is not confined to responding to need. A pastor has opportunities that are often not available to other professionals. The pastoral ministry takes place within a setting (both the congregation and the geographical area) which provides occasions for the pastor to mix and work with a considerable number of people who do not present themselves as 'clients' (even if some of them are just as much in need of help as those who have actually recognized their needs). What sort of pastoral ministry might be offered in this context, so that people can be nurtured and encouraged in their natural growth and development, and in their relationships and attitudes towards others? How can people be helped to reflect upon themselves – in the light of the earlier definition – within 'psychological, ethical and theological frames of reference'?

There are undoubtedly many ways in which the pastoral ministry already encourages such reflection amongst congregations and in the neighbourhood. People are helped to grow in understanding through Lent courses and house-groups, where matters of spiritual and social concern can be discussed in personal terms, and not simply as 'academic' subjects. Spiritual direction, which is practised in different styles, preaching and teaching, enable Christians to develop in faith and understanding. It is possible that some of the questions and issues raised in this book will provide food for thought in discussion groups, ideas for inclusion in preaching and teaching, and a psychological background for spiritual direction.

As an educator of adults myself, I do not wish to devalue

any of these ways of helping people to grow. However, my concern is that knowledge is not just *about* faith, doctrine or church order, or *about* personal and social issues. While all these matters are clearly part of the development of a mature Christian, the danger of teaching, or indeed of certain kinds of learning, is that it provides head-knowledge alone. While intellectual development is important and a more mature understanding of faith, social and political issues is to be encouraged in the religious life, maturity consists of more than knowledge. Faith consists of more than learning about credal definitions or biblical texts. The 'heart' is as important as the 'head'. Personal development is not confined to learning information, any more than personality can simply be defined by reference to a person's IQ. Here the links between my material and spirituality are obvious, since a spiritual person is not one who knows about God, but who knows God; and levels of maturity within and between people rise when they can share with each other not what they know, but who they are, what they think, and how they feel.

Within the religious life indeed, the heart is just as important as the head, which is why the term 'conversion' has been important in Christian tradition. Whether that conversion be, in Hopkins' words, 'at a crash' like Paul or 'a lingering-out sweet skill' like Augustine[7] (and it will be clear from later chapters that I particularly lean towards the latter), emotional development, in all its complexity, is even more important for personal growth in faith than intellectual development. Indeed, the American person-centred therapist Carl Rogers[8] has argued that learning which involves any change to the self is often threatening and is resisted, despite the reasonableness of the arguments. Changes in attitudes may be a necessary precursor to changes in thinking. C. S. Lewis provides a good example of this in his children's story, where Aslan describes the dwarfs who cannot see a glorious feast set out in front of them: 'Their prison is only in their minds, yet they are in that prison; and so afraid of being taken in that they cannot be taken out.'[9] Some people cannot accept an almost water-tight statement, because it would require them to let go of the security of their fixed beliefs. Their minds cannot be opened, partly because a change of mind would affect their whole selves. This is as true of people within our churches as outside them. People who look for security through black and white answers are often unable to accept more subtle ways of understanding. Yet subtlety and discrimination are necessary for exploring and understanding the complexities of the world, of belief, and indeed of other people.

If emotional attitudes govern the way people see things, education in the pastoral ministry needs to be sympathetic to and aware of the difficulties which might be encountered. If useful learning is to take place about faith, about personal and social problems, and about the other matters of concern to the Christian, promotion and encouragement of attitudinal change may be just as important as imparting information. This is especially important in helping people find a more mature faith, since the questioning that is involved in such a personal quest can involve as much uncomfortable heart-searching as puzzling head-scratching. All such changes and developments will, I believe, be considerably helped, when people belong to an open-minded and caring group, which itself grows and matures. Development may be possible in some small groups that is not possible in the context of the congregation as a whole.

In emphasizing the need for the development of the heart, or of the emotional life, as well as of other kinds of knowledge, including Christian faith, there is support from the letter to the Corinthians; Paul too is suspicious not just of knowledge, but also of certain types of faith (such as that which can move mountains), and he writes that without love all this is nothing.[10] To help people to develop emotionally – that is, to be able to love – may be just as important as developing people's knowledge and faith. Facilitating people's faith may then begin by helping them to understand themselves. And if Paul leaves us in no doubt that the most important aspect is love, even the capacity to love (which in some churches is rather glibly talked and preached about) is far from simple, because there are many other feelings which stand in the way of its expression. How can pastoral ministry assist the development of *emotional* health and maturity alongside the development of a more loving faith?

It is, of course, possible to tackle this dimension of life –

the development of the individual – through explicit teaching and preaching, or through group discussions. I am aware that courses in pastoral counselling, for example, often teach people as much about themselves as they do about how to help others. In the parish, programmes to train lay visitors in listening skills or grief work often perform the same function. These types of training group, where the learning is often experiential, and which encourage people to open up some of their thoughts and feelings to each other, develop much more than 'head-knowledge'. Another example is Marriage Enrichment, an enterprise which amply demonstrates (even though the numbers attending are small) that there is certainly as much room in pastoral care for helping people and relationships to grow, as there is for working with tense, unhappy or broken situations. Marriage Enrichment is much more than a preventive measure – it is an opportunity to deepen partnerships which are already satisfactory enough. But I wonder whether there might also be a place for Faith Enrichment, with similar groups where people can say what they feel, and be honest about what they think, without fear of being labelled heretical?

Growth through Pastoral Presence

Pastoral care can assist, therefore, the growth and development of different groups of people: through helping some of them in crisis situations; through assisting others to grow at times of celebration in life-changes; through providing educational programmes or discussion groups of one kind or another for others; and through the traditional forms of ministry, preaching, teaching and spiritual direction. If one of the main aims of the pastoral ministry is to enable persons to become more mature and to reach towards the fullness of Christ, such a high priority must involve many different ways of working towards the same goal. I am in fact not over concerned here with particular techniques whereby this important aim might be achieved. My major concern is to share some of the insights about stages of life which are currently available, and in particular to allow some models of psychological development to rub shoulders with some models of faith development. With the exception of a few asides, I consider these life themes as providing a background that can inform all pastoral care, rather than a set of instructions on 'how to do it'.

In an earlier book[11] I have attempted to show the relevance of life stages to the detailed work of the counsellor. Much of that book, particularly the appendices, could similarly inform the work of pastoral care, although I concentrate there upon psycho-social development alone. Here I am much more interested in the relevance of life stages as they are related to the development of faith and meaning. Campbell[12] refers to 'The Journey' as a metaphor for the quest of faith. 'Each of us,' he writes,' has a pilgrimage to make on a road which is strangely familiar, though we know we have never trodden it before.' My attempt in the last four chapters of this book to sketch out the themes that occur in personal development, aims to help the pastor identify where people might be on their 'journey' through life, even though no two journeys will ever be the same. With such understanding it may then be possible, even in the most informal of contacts and the most casual of conversations, for there to be opportunities of nurturing signs of change and of movement in personal and in faith attitudes. But another equally important reason for sketching these themes is to help pastors themselves to look at their own development, and at ways of being with people that in itself helps promotes development towards maturity.

Pastoral ministry is as much about *being* as it is about *doing*. The psychological, ethical and faith attitudes of the pastor, in casual conversations as well as in preaching, speak as loudly as actions do. It is in little ways that we promote or hold back other people's growth and development. Just as parents can enhance or undermine the development of their children as much by who they are as by what they actually say, and as much by the way they handle situations as by the particular values which they express; so in pastoral care, attitudes, unspoken values and ways of approaching issues are as influential in moulding the development of others for good or ill, as the actual gospel which the pastor teaches or proclaims. Like it or not, a pastor, like any 'authority figure', becomes a model – sometimes a good model, sometimes a bad model, but probably a mixture of the two. He or she is often seen as a person whom some people want to emulate, or whom others react against. If the pastor is perceived as someone who is striving to understand what being human involves, and as a person who seeks (though does not always find) a more mature, more whole way of being, this will help build up others into the 'fullness of Christ'.

In comparing the pastoral ministry to parenting, although on a larger and more complex scale, I am reminded of the psychoanalyst D. W. Winnicott's description of the task of parents as one of promoting personal growth in their offspring. He writes that children and adolescents will 'not be contented to find anything but the whole of themselves'.[13] His phrase 'anything but the whole' bears remarkable similarities to the New English Bible's expression, 'nothing less than the full', in its translation of the verse from which I have taken my title: 'So shall we all at last attain to the unity inherent in our faith and our knowledge of the Son of God – to mature manhood, measured by nothing less than the full stature of Christ.'[14]

This close relationship between the movement towards the fullness of Christ, and the development of personality is further underlined by the references in New Testament to the contrast between the child and the mature person. Paul writes in the letter to the Corinthians of having to grow up from being a child, and having to put away the child's outlook and thoughts.[15] In the letter to the Ephesians the passage goes on: 'We are no longer to be children, tossed by the waves and whirled about by every fresh gust . . .'[16] So too, in the development of maturity, some of the feelings and phantasies of the child, that linger on in the adult, need to be reappraised for their truth and relevance and set aside as no longer appropriate. At the same time, if the Gospels appear to contradict the Epistles by emphasizing the value of becoming as a little child, they do in fact balance the picture, because some features that are present in the child (such as spontaneity, the freedom to play, and openness to the immediacy of present experience and feeling) can easily be forced underground by parental strictures, depriving the later adult of much that is healthy and good.

Some aspects of childhood therefore have to be put away,

but others recovered if we are to grow into the fullness of Christ. The pastoral ministry can help foster the milieu in which growing and becoming can take place, as surely as it can inhibit it. The Church has demonstrated many different types of parenting in its history, from the caring, forgiving and accepting parent on the one hand, responding sensitively to individual persons in distress, to the severely critical or over-protective parent on the other, preaching do's and don't's to all and sundry. But parenting, educating, shepherding (there are a variety of images for the pastoral role), particularly of those who are in chronological age quite old enough to look after themselves, does not always involve an active approach. It is often through presence, through casual conversations, and through example that both children and adults are helped to grow in wisdom and maturity.

Difficult though this task may be, I am the last person to want to counsel perfection, and I have no wish to place even greater demands upon pastors than they already have imposed upon them (or impose upon themselves). There can never be a perfect pastor, just as there are no perfect parents. Winnicott used the phrase 'good enough' of parenting, a phrase which attracts, not because it suggests complacency on the one hand, or tortured striving to do the right thing on the other, but because it affirms one's efforts *to be*. Reflecting on or charting the paths towards maturity is not an attempt to describe perfection or sanctity, or even to make so bold as to define what 'the fullness of Christ' actually is. I deliberately choose to qualify my title with the word '*Towards* the Fullness of Christ'. The ideas upon which I draw, as well as my own thinking, are time-bound and culture-bound, and the definitions of the stages of life, and what makes for maturity, inevitably reflect something of the spirit of our post-Freudian psychological age. Throughout development there is always a transitory quality, although I prefer to use the more positive term 'transition'.

Nor are my views on mature faith and personality development, which inevitably contain a subjective element, intended to be taken as a self-portrait. Like the reader, I am aware of how much growing there is to do in life, whatever one's age, and I can think of little worse than deliberately striving to be a saint! What seems more important is to be as fully human and as fully divine (in the sense that we are made in the image of God) as we can be, whatever stage of life we are in, and to whatever extent our individual capacities enable us to develop.

To be as fully human and as fully divine is to be as Christ-like as possible, at every stage of life. There are some who may be dismissive of psychological models, and who hold out in their place the supreme and ultimate model of Christ. What we need, they say, is to follow as closely as we can his example towards maturity, knowing that his Spirit is in us, guiding and supporting us along the way.

People who say this may find it helpful for themselves. I have to say that I do not, especially when exploring the complex subject of wholeness and maturity. I have to ask which picture of Christ I am to follow to provide me with the model of maturity? Jesus is as much a figure for personal projections of our own wishes and prejudices as are the figures of God the Father, or indeed the Holy Spirit, in whose name people have performed not only the best but also the most dreadful of deeds. So which Jesus is to be our model? Some will emphasize his compassion, others his rigorous demands (witness church debates on divorce or homosexuality), yet others his freedom from legalism; some will emphasize his teaching and his directiveness, others his capacity to listen and say little or simply to ask questions; some his messianic role and his anger in the face of corruption, others his more passive role as the victim of oppression. The quest for a psychological analysis of Jesus is as likely to end up with the individual psychologist's Jesus as the quest for the historical Jesus has been said to tell us more about the individual historian's Jesus. The Gospels, the nearest we get to an objective record, provide us with tantalizing glimpses, none of which should ever be taken to represent the whole Jesus.

We could, of course, take these different interpretations, and combine them in search of a comprehensive model to guide us in our exploration of maturity and wholeness. To do so may bring us nearer to a more complete picture in which our projections can be confronted. To do so, however, would be to confine the model of Jesus to the historical person of the Gospels, and to rely overmuch upon biblical criticism to sort out the wheat from the chaff. To concentrate upon the historical figure is to neglect that other vital part of Christian teaching, both the pre-existent Logos and the risen Christ, where we move beyond history and enter the realm of symbol. It is only by beginning to transcend the human and the historical, that we reach towards greater expression of the fullness of Christ.[17] It is this towards which I press in the latter part of this book but, before arriving at that point, I need to look first at the more mundane, at all too human examples of the stages of personal and faith development.

It may be that the models which different psychologists have outlined help us to see new aspects of the historical Jesus and the transcendent figure of Christ. They certainly need testing out against real lives, not only of Jesus but also of the other towering figures in the history of faith, Western and Eastern. It is, I hope, in the very process of searching for understanding of what is meant by 'the fullness of Christ' and 'mature personhood' that we are edged a little nearer to the sense of fulfilment and wholeness that many of us would like to understand and, at least occasionally, to achieve.

1. This definition is taken from 'Defining Pastoral Psychotherapy' by C. R. Schlauch (*The Journal of Pastoral Care*, XXXIX, 3, 1985).
2. Rom. 8:29.
3. Luke 17:21.
4. J. W. Fowler, *Faith Development and Pastoral Care* (Fortress Press 1987), ch. 5. See also B. Reed, *The Dynamics of Religion* (Darton, Longman and Todd 1978). Reed describes the ways in which congregations can promote or inhibit healthy religious and personal development.
5. D. Capps, *Life Cycle Theory and Pastoral Care* (Fortress Press 1983), ch. 3.
6. W. Carr, *Brief Encounters* (SPCK 1985).
7. From 'The Wreck of the Deutschland' by Gerard Manley Hopkins, in W. H. Gardner (ed.), *Gerard Manley Hopkins: a Selection of His Poems and Prose* (Penguin 1953).
8. C. Rogers, *Freedom to Learn* (Ohio, Merrill, 1969), chs. 7 and 8.
9. C. S. Lewis, *The Last Battle* (Penguin 1964), p. 135.
10. 1 Cor. 13:3.

11. M. Jacobs, *The Presenting Past* (Open University Press 1986).
12. A. V. Campbell, *Rediscovering Pastoral Care* (Darton Longman and Todd, rev. edn 1986), pp. 82–97. Campbell is using a universal image here, one which recurs throughout mythology as well as in writing about spirituality. Thus the journey is a significant part of the Epic of Gilgamesh. The stories about Abraham, the Israelites in the wilderness, and in the New Testament perhaps the journey to Jerusalem are all of a piece. In later Christian tradition Bunyan's *Pilgrim's Progress* is well known, and amongst recent authors who use the idea there is Christopher Bryant's *The Heart in Pilgrimage* (Darton Longman and Todd 1980) or G. Hughes' *The God of Surprises* (Darton Longman and Todd 1985).
13. D. W. Winnicott, *Playing and Reality* (Penguin 1974), p. 168.
14. Eph. 4:13.
15. 1 Cor. 13:11.
16. Eph. 4:14 (NEB).
17. There are parallels to this essential idea in Eastern religion, to which I refer in the last chapter. Buddha was, of course, an historical person too, but this does not prevent a Zen master from writing 'the real Buddha has no mouth and preaches no Dharma' (a deliberately ambiguous term which means, variously, 'properties', 'teachings', 'true facts', 'real events', etc.). D. E. Harding, *On Having No Head* (London and New York, Arkana, 1986), p. 25.

2

Models

Simplifying Complexities

There are some aspects of human development which are relatively easy to describe, although there is always a danger of forcing the complexities of life into rigid categories. Physical development, for instance, is fairly standard, so that obstetricians can plot the progress of a pregnancy to within a few days, while paediatricians can assess height, weight and various physical signs and skills and, by using a set of norms, determine whether or not a child's development is satisfactory. Chronological age is a fair predictor of body development, with clear changes, for example, in childhood and puberty and, after the peak of physical maturity in early adulthood, the predictable changes that come with ageing. Yet even in respect of physical development, due allowance has to be made for the variations in the speed at which individual children and young people develop, and at which individual older people begin to lose some of their physical and mental abilities. Variables such as genetic inheritance, diet and standards of living, as well as certain psychological factors mean that norms can provide us with rough guides, but never with precise information about any one individual.

Rather less predictable, sometimes controversial, but nevertheless still sufficiently objective to be helpful in the work of educationalists and of psychologists are norms for mental development. By this I mean the development of language, thinking and intelligence, and the co-ordination of brain and body. IQ tests, and other means of measuring psychological skills and predispositions, are again based on standardized norms, although such norms are not universal and have to be arrived at for different sets of people, different ages, and different cultural and family backgrounds. The work of Jean Piaget[1] was particularly concerned with stages in the development of thinking. His theories have been useful to those who have studied the development of thinking about religious ideas. Goldman's[2] research into the stages of religious ideas and images in childhood and adolescence was influential in the 1960s, and gave rise to new designs for teaching material in schools and churches. Fowler,[3] whose research into faith development appears later in this chapter, has also integrated Piaget's ideas into his own scheme.

There is, however, criticism of Piaget's use of the term 'stages' to describe cognitive development. Critics have said that the many influences on a child make it impossible to produce the same stage of development in every child at a given age. The term 'stage' has therefore to be qualified so that it allows room for the fact that children pass through the sequence of stages at different rates. It is also important to recognize that earlier stages of thinking are not altogether lost as a child moves into the next developmental stage. These essential and necessary qualifications are equally relevant when attempting to chart (as I do in this chapter) the even more complex emotional, moral and faith developments of children and adults.

There are so many variables that influence personality development that it is essential to understand that no two people are identical. This is, of course, true also of everyone's physical nature; there are both common features and distinct differences in appearance. Similarly, in the maturation of the whole person, nearly everyone passes through common stages of development, but with particular features at every turn, with the result that as individuals we not only resemble others in broad terms, but we are at every moment experiencing ourselves, others and the world around us in unique ways. This shared humanity and yet individual distinctiveness and preciousness is seen in the teaching of both Jesus and Paul. While it makes sense, therefore, to attempt to describe common experiences and to chart the development of persons towards maturity, equal recognition has to be given to the different circumstances and the specific causes that colour individual reactions and responses.

In order to describe what may be common experiences, even if they are expressed at the same time in infinite variations, it is helpful to adopt a model of human development. Complex issues require more simple models, to help us to chart where we are. However, here is a cautionary note to anticipate further cautions expressed in the next chapter: if a simplified model is mistaken for that which it attempts to represent, it ceases to be valuable. Fortunately we are saved from mistaking the model for the whole person, because there are several models of development, each of which has its own emphasis. It is highly unlikely that any one of them is complete in itself and that the others are wrong. In fact, the different models also have several features in common, which become clearer as they are placed together. In this chapter I use several models of 'stages of life' and try to bring their various dimensions together into a rather more detailed and complete chart of the movement towards maturity, one that includes 'psychological, ethical and theological frames of reference'.[4] Perhaps the most interesting feature in common is that most of the models tend towards some kind of ideal of wholeness, which means that views of psychological maturity share much with the religious ideal of achieving 'the fullness of Christ'.

Jung

Although in many respects Jung is not the easiest of writers to start with, his model of human development has a useful simplicity to it, which makes for a straightforward beginning. Fordham, in her introduction to Jung's thought,[5] writes that it was important to Jung to differentiate between what he calls the 'stages of life', and in her book this differentiation is straightforward in that these stages appear to consist of a first and a second half of life. The first half of life, up to the midpoint of 35–40 years of age is concerned with establishing oneself, through marriage, building a family, and developing the skills necessary for a career. It is essentially an outward-looking period.

The second half of life is more concerned with an inward journey, with understanding oneself, with finding new meaning and purpose, and above all with the process Jung

Childhood	Youth (13–40)	Mid-life	Old Age
First half of life (Establishing)		Second half of life (Individuation)	

Figure 1: Jung's Stages of Life

called 'individuation'. Individuation links in well with my theme, since it is essentially the finding of wholeness, in which those aspects of the personality that may have been neglected earlier in life, or that have been repressed in order to make one's way in the world, now need to be reclaimed. Individuation does not mean becoming ego-centred or individualistic, but rather describes a process of becoming more aware both of one's uniqueness, and of one's relationship to 'all living things, even with inorganic matter and the cosmos itself'.[6] In Jung's thought, one of the archetypes of wholeness is the self, and one of the symbols of the self is Christ.

Such a description accords well with the presence in many of our churches of more people in the second than in the first half of life, since religion speaks to this quest for meaning. It should not, however, be taken to mean that individuation only begins in the second half of life, or that dimensions from the first half of life cease to be relevant (work, family relationships, sexuality all continue to play an important part for most people). In fact Fordham's description of two halves of life is misleading, because Jung divided life into four stages, childhood, youth and young adulthood, mid-life and old age. Samuels'[7] very helpful guide to Jungian and post-Jungian thought and practice points out that a major strength of Jung is that he was a 'whole of life psychologist'. Samuels himself is concerned about the idea of stages of life suggesting a linear process or progression through separate stages – a necessary qualification to which I shall return.

Jung's concentration on the second half of life was partly a personal reaction to Freud's emphasis on the first half of life. He wished to give a more positive place to the problem of religion as opposed to Freud's important exposure of the problem of sexuality. Yet it would be a mistake to see such a relatively simple model of two, or four, stages of life as representing a simple psychology. Individuation is a life-long process, 'a tortuous and slippery path'.[8] Furthermore Jung's interest in the second half of life did not mean that he dismissed outright Freud's analysis of childhood development. As I will show, these can still be fitted into a composite model alongside Jung's four stages and two halves of life.

Levinson

A similar four-stage model of the seasons of life, but with some useful additions, is found in the writing of Daniel Levinson, whose work is another of the influences on Fowler's research into faith development.[9] Unlike Jung, Levinson is not concerned with religion, although he adopts the same image which religious writing often does when he describes life as a journey that 'follows an underlying universal pattern on which there are endless cultural and individual variations'.[10] The four seasons of life are divided into twenty-year periods, but perhaps the most important feature of his scheme is that between each of the main divisions there is a transitional period, where life needs to be 'fundamentally re-examined, assessed and modified'.[11]

These transitional periods emphasize that the stages of life are not cut and dried divisions into which a person moves at particular dates and definite ages. In the more detailed plan that appears in Levinson's work, each of the main central blocks are also divided into shorter periods, with further transitional points. *Passing Through Transitions* is the name of another book on the phases of adult life,[12] and its title underlines the continuous movement that we would expect to be involved in the terms 'growth and development'. The author

<table>
<tr><td rowspan="2">JUNG</td><td colspan="2">Childhood</td><td colspan="2">Youth (13–40)</td><td colspan="2">Mid-life</td><td>Old Age</td></tr>
<tr><td colspan="4">First half of life
(Establishing)</td><td colspan="3">Second half of life
(Individuation)</td></tr>
<tr><td rowspan="2">LEVINSON</td><td colspan="2">0–20
Childhood and
Adolescence</td><td colspan="2">21–40
Early
Adulthood</td><td colspan="2">41–60
Mid Adulthood</td><td>65+
Late
Adulthood</td></tr>
<tr><td></td><td>Transition
(17–22)</td><td></td><td>Transition
(40–45)</td><td></td><td>Transition
(60–65)</td><td></td></tr>
</table>

Figure 2: Levinson added to the chart

is also careful to distinguish between men's and women's experience of transitions, as indeed Levinson has done. I return to some of these gender issues and differences in chapters 3 and 6.

Freud and Faber

Freud's main area of concern in terms of developmental psychology was childhood, even though the majority of his patients were adult. It was in childhood that he looked both for the reasons for neurotic or distorted development, and the foundations of adult maturity. Consequently his stages of life look rather imbalanced, with five stages up to and including adolescence, and with adulthood lumped together in one unit. Freud's pessimism about the value of analysis to people in the later stages of life, on the grounds of their being too fixed in their ways to be able to benefit from it, or to make changes, has been shown to be unfounded in the developments of therapy and counselling. Indeed Freud is a poor example of his own pessimism, since he himself initiated his ideas in his forties, and went on developing them into his seventies! If he has a view of adult development, it is based more upon the analytic process itself, whereby men and women can grow in understanding and maturity, away from the inhibiting factors that have stayed with them from their childhood experience. Self-analysis, such as Freud practised throughout his life, has some resemblances to the spiritual discipline of self-examination, although the latter sometimes has a self-condemning rather than a self-analytical quality. Self-reflection is perhaps a better word to describe what might be the common factor in the psychoanalytic and the spiritual paths towards mature personal development. It is a feature of old age in particular that, given the stimulus and the interest of others, old people continue to develop as whole persons through self-reflection, right through to the point of death.

Nevertheless, it is Freud's concentration on the first twenty years of life that has made the most impact upon Western thinking. His ideas, however, are relevant to the whole of human development and not just to the understanding of children, because he has shown that adults can regress to childhood stages or remain fixated in them. Although this may seem to be of more interest to psychopathology and pastoral counselling, by expanding terms like regression and fixation to include non-neurotic functions, it is possible to say (as Freud himself did) that *all* adults (and not just those who have problems) go on carrying their child within them, both in positive as well as negative ways. This child influences the way they think and behave. It is for this reason that familiarity with childhood patterns of thought and reaction provides a useful entrance to the understanding of various stages of adult life.

Freud's overriding interest in the early developmental stages means that the left-hand side of our chart has to be stretched to accommodate the four divisions of childhood. The next diagram is therefore an enlarged detail of the first twenty or so years of human development:

<table>
<tr><td rowspan="2">JUNG</td><td colspan="4">Childhood</td><td>Youth (13–40)</td></tr>
<tr><td colspan="5">First half of life (Establishing)</td></tr>
<tr><td>LEVINSON</td><td colspan="4">Childhood and Adolescence
(0–20)</td><td>Transition
(17–22)</td></tr>
<tr><td>FREUD</td><td>Oral
(0–1)</td><td>Anal
(1–3)</td><td>Genital
(3–6)</td><td>Latency
(5–12)</td><td>Adolescence
(12–25)</td></tr>
</table>

Figure 3: Freud added to the chart

Were it not for the innovative nature of Freud's model, and the direct use made of it by the Dutch pastoral theologian Heije Faber, I might have been tempted to pass over the somewhat narrow interpretation of childhood development, in favour of Erikson's more comprehensive and expansive model of the stages of life. Freud concentrated upon the pleasurable zones of the body – the mouth, anus and genitals – as moulding the development of a child's personality. In his own work, and in those who have followed him, equal importance in fact has to be attached to the relationship between child and parent, albeit based upon feeding, toilet-training, and incipient sexuality. The terms 'oral, anal and genital' need to be understood as symbols, or shorthand words, to describe features of personality and of relationships to others which have definite links with, but are not exclusively limited to, bodily functions. It is possible to talk of the oral character, the anal character, and the genital character. I have myself used the first three stages of childhood to demonstrate the way they are pervasive through all the other stages of life, although I prefer to describe the first three stages as the 'Oral/Dependency/Trust Stage', the 'Anal/Authority/Autonomy Stage' and the 'Genital/Oedipal/Social/Competitive/Co-operative Stage'.[13] I introduce features of these stages as major life themes in later chapters.

Faber[14] examines religious images, thinking and behaviour using the three childhood stages and adolescence, confining his analysis to these types of religion: oral religion, anal religion, genital religion, and adolescent religion. In subsequent chapters I include Faber's descriptions in more detail. Oral characteristics (trust and dependency issues) clearly form an important part of religious faith and experience, and are especially seen in primitive religion. Anal characteristics (rules, authority, punishment) are equally evident both in individual expressions of faith and in legalistic religion. The area of sexuality is one with which traditional Christianity has generally been less than comfortable, although in a book on models of God, McFague[15] reminds us that in addition to models of God as Father and Mother (each of which has links with anal and oral stages respectively), some of the mystics speak of God as a lover and integrate eroticism with their spirituality. She also uses the metaphor of God as 'friend'. This image tallies with the Freudian view that successful resolution of the genital stage involves breaking away from parents (and therefore perhaps from parental images of God). The Oedipal ties to parents are replaced, although probably not until the child becomes adult, by feelings of respect for and friendship with parents, by a close sexual relationship being made outside the family, and by engaging in relationships with others which are 'aim-inhibited', where sexuality is sublimated. In theological terms *eros* is sublimated into *philia* and *agape*. McFague's different metaphors, coming from a feminist theological perspective, seem to accord with Freud's understanding of mature relationships.

Erikson and Capps

Erik Erikson[16] developed a model which he called 'The Eight Ages of Man', a phrase which is more indicative of the time when he wrote than of any conscious disregard of women. (Nevertheless, questions need to be borne in mind about the applicability to both men and women of what he and others write, given that the models I use here have been suggested by men.) Erikson not only extended the stages to include three ages of adult life, which I illustrate below. He also suggested that each stage of life brings with it special developmental tasks, which are sometimes resolved well, and sometimes badly. For most people the resolution is probably a mixture of positive and negative resolution. In the 'oral stage' therefore, Erikson proposes that the issue which has to be worked through is one of learning to trust in mother, in the small world encompassing the baby, and through such trust to have faith in one's own being. This stage lays the foundation for trust and faith in the succeeding stages of life. I will show in chapter 4 how this idea is supported by other writers.

If there is a failure in nurturing, be it accidental or deliberate, the outcome for the baby is likely to be one of mistrust, an inability to believe either in others or in one's basic self. Such an outcome inevitably weakens the facility with which a person copes with the developmental tasks of the next stage, where physical developments necessitate dealing with new issues. In this stage the term 'anal' is expanded by Erikson to include muscular control in general. In the 'muscular-anal' stage the issue that has to be resolved is one of autonomy versus shame and doubt. Freud's first five life stages in Figure 3 can therefore be filled out by including Erikson's bi-polar terms which describe the strengths or weaknesses that may result from each of the stages illustrated in Figure 4.

Two concerns may have been raised in the reader's mind. It seems rash to assert that a toddler of three years old achieves autonomy, or that at any of these stages the strength or weakness is fixed for ever. That is true, and it is more important to read the terms as expressing basic issues that arise at each stage, but which are not resolved (and perhaps never completely resolved) until later in life. Furthermore,

JUNG	Childhood				Youth (13–40)
	First half of life (Establishing)				
LEVINSON	Childhood and Adolescence (0–20)				Transition (17–22)
FREUD	Oral (0–1)	Anal (1–3)	Genital (3–6)	Latency (5–12)	Adolescence (12–25)
(Strength)	Trust	Autonomy	Initiative	Industry	Identity
ERIKSON	*vs*	*vs*	*vs*	*vs*	*vs*
(Weakness)	Mistrust	Shame	Guilt	Inferiority	Confusion

Figure 4: The first five stages: Erikson's additions

under stress an apparent strength may give way to its underlying opposite. I look at this issue as one of the cautions in the next chapter.

The reader's other concern may be that while the strengths are clearly desirable qualities, and most of the weaknesses we would rather do without, surely there are some aspects of the weaknesses, such as guilt, which are important? One of the criticisms raised against Freudian thinking is that it appears to try to get rid of guilt. Surely people might treat each other better if they took more notice of their guilty feelings? This familiar question hides the difference between realistic guilt and neurotic guilt, and between guilt and concern, an issue which I briefly address in chapter 6. Concern is a much more positive basis for relationships than fear of conscience and guilt. True concern for others involves selfless regard for them and what they are experiencing. It is a more constructive motive for right behaviour than the more negative deterrent of behaving towards others so as not to offend one's punitive conscience. Kohlberg's analysis of moral development, integrated into the chart at the end of this chapter, helps to clarify this issue.

Since Erikson carries the Eight Ages into adult life as well, the second half of our chart of the stages of life can be expanded to include the three phases of adulthood. It will be seen that Erikson, like Jung, places emphasis on the task of integration in the last stage, although he views this as starting chronologically later than Jung does. In fact, actual ages tend to limit the usefulness of the different models. Intimate relationships (Erikson, stage 6) can be made in the late teens, or might not be entered into until well into middle age. So too the years of parenthood stretch over many years, even if for one person or couple the family only remains twenty or thirty years in the parental home. The ages included in Figure 5 have to be taken as very rough indicators. Because there are all kinds of limitations in using chronological ages in such models, I omit most of these apparent 'norms' after this figure.

	Youth (13–40)	Mid-life	Old Age
JUNG	First half of life (Establishing)	Second half of life (Individuation)	
LEVINSON	21–40 Early Adulthood	41–60 Mid Adulthood	65+ Late Adulthood
	Transition (40–45)	Transition (60–65)	
Age	Young Adulthood (16–22)	Mid Adulthood (25–55)	Maturity (55+)
(Strength)	Intimacy	Generativity/Creativity	Integrity
ERIKSON	*vs*	*vs*	*vs*
(Weakness)	Isolation	Stagnation	Despair

Figure 5: Adding Erikson's Stages of Adult Life

Erikson has also suggested that each of the stages of individual development contains factors which contribute to a more healthy society. Faith and religion are related to the oral stage, law and justice to the anal stage, the importance of role to the genital stage and so on.[17] This is not the only reference to the importance of religion in Erikson, who also wrote fascinating psycho-biographies about Luther and Gandhi.[18] Erikson's work is drawn upon with some frequency in American literature, and applied to different aspects of pastoral care and ministry.[19]

Typical of this use of Erikson is Capps' study of the relevance to pastoral care of his model of the Eight Ages and his life-cycle theory.[20] It is particularly interesting for those who value Erikson's work, since Capps' book arises partly from personal conversations with him on his understandings of religion. Capps' attempt to link the 'weaknesses' and the 'strengths' of each age with the seven deadly sins and with Christian virtues is interesting, but is somewhat contrived, and adds little to either set of moral terms. It is more relevant here to draw attention to his chapter on ritual and life-cycle theory, since this raises interesting possibilities for the pastoral ministry, demonstrating that Erikson's ideas need not be confined to pastoral counselling.

By 'ritual' Capps and Erikson do not simply mean sacred rites and ceremonies, but also the social rituals which form part of the life of a community. Capps emphasizes the latter meaning and relates it to the parish, showing how ministry can foster the rituals of everyday life, which themselves enhance shared religious meanings. Different forms of ritual are typical of each of the Eight Ages. Thus the numinous aspect of ritual is connected with the first age, the oral stage. In sacred rites the numinous often involves the act of looking or being looked upon. In some ceremonies only the priest is allowed to enter the Holy of Holies – although this may actually heighten the sense of the numinous in those who are not permitted to 'see'. In other ceremonies the act of looking is encouraged, for example, in the elevation of the host, the use of sacred icons and images, all of which help the sense of the numinous, both in looking and being looked upon.

This sense of the numinous is closely linked by Erikson to the relationship between mother and baby, which also involves gazing, responding to, and being looked and smiled upon. The act of looking is a vital means of communicating feelings, because in this pre-verbal stage words are meaningless except as expressing tones of voice, which may convey kind or cross feelings in the parent. It is seeing and being seen which helps overcome the baby's fear of separation and isolation; and in religion too, although the numinous in one sense suggests a distance between the worshipper and the god, it is the numinous aspect of ritual which also helps overcome a person's sense of isolation from their god.

Ritualization in Erikson is thus positive, although he also

describes a more negative form, which he calls 'ritual excess'. This tends to lead to poor social relationships and to false religion. There is an equivalent ritual excess for each of the eight forms of ritualization. In his idea of ritual excess Erikson is in some agreement with Freud, who was himself very critical of religious ritual, comparing it to obsessional actions.[21] One example of ritual excess is idolatry, the reverse side of the numinous in the oral stage. Although Erikson refers here to idolatry in religious terms, with objects being treated like gods, there is an equivalent idolatry in human relationships, known as idolizing or idealizing. Not only do objects or people take the place of the numinous, but also in psychological terms, the effect of idealization is to weaken rather than strengthen the sense of self, and to dwell more upon the gap between oneself and another. Idealization of another is invariably at the idealizer's expense.

In pastoral ministry, and in the community life of the parish, Capps highlights the value of the recognition of people, as being the equivalent numinous ritual in socialization. The pastor needs to lead the way in seeing persons as individuals, and in encouraging people to recognize and affirm each other's distinctiveness. 'There is a sense in which the pastor needs to function like the mother in the mother-infant relationship because pastors are mediators of the presence of God.'[22]

The numinous stage provides a good example of the way in which Capps uses the Erikson scheme. It is not necessary to expand any further here upon the other ritual functions of the pastor and of parish life in the building up of the Body of Christ, although the chapter 'The Ritual Co-ordinator' in Capp's book is worth exploring, even if some of the other links he makes are rather less valuable. Like Capps, I also want to avoid suggesting 'specific initiatives' that might follow from the application of such models to pastoral care. Yet the discriminating application of such a psychological model to pastoral care, which Capps demonstrates, provides a valuable example of the way understanding of psychological development can enhance the pastoral ministry.[23]

Piaget and Cognitive Thinking: Tillich and Faith

I am not aware that Tillich was influenced by Piaget, although it is clear that psychoanalytic theory (particularly as developed by Fromm and the neo-Freudians) was important to him. I bring these two names together because Piaget's theories of the development of thinking have given rise to research into types of religious thinking, which seem to me to show parallels to Tillich's analysis of types of faith. Both Piaget and Tillich also provide a way into introducing Fowler's model of faith development.

In my earlier reference to Piaget I suggested the difficulty of using the term 'stage' to describe development. Without wishing to deter the reader by introducing superfluous technical terms, it is helpful to set out the stages in which Piaget described levels of selecting, organizing and co-ordinating experience, because it is partly this which religious faith also tries to do. I therefore add the Piagetian stages (with the approximate ages he gives) and the first two of Tillich's types of world-view, to the chart:

<table>
<tr><td rowspan="2">JUNG</td><td colspan="6">Childhood</td><td colspan="4">Youth</td></tr>
<tr><td colspan="10">First half of life (Establishing)</td></tr>
<tr><td>LEVINSON</td><td colspan="9">Childhood and Adolescence</td><td>Transition</td></tr>
<tr><td>FREUD</td><td>Oral</td><td colspan="2">Anal</td><td colspan="2">Genital</td><td colspan="3">Latency</td><td colspan="2">Adolescence</td></tr>
<tr><td>ERIKSON</td><td>Trust
vs
Mistrust</td><td colspan="2">Autonomy
vs
Shame</td><td colspan="2">Initiative
vs
Guilt</td><td colspan="3">Industry
vs
Inferiority</td><td colspan="2">Identity
vs
Confusion</td></tr>
<tr><td>PIAGET</td><td colspan="2">0–2
sensori-motor
intelligence</td><td colspan="2">2–7
intuitive
thinking</td><td colspan="3">7–11
concrete
thinking</td><td colspan="3">11+
abstract
thinking</td></tr>
<tr><td>TILLICH</td><td colspan="4">World-View A
pre-conscious
literalism</td><td colspan="6">World-view B
conscious
literalism</td></tr>
</table>

Figure 6: Adding Piaget and Tillich

The first two years involve elementary patterns of dealing with external objects, of differentiating one from another, and of learning that they exist apart from the child's own perception of them. Although this stage may seem irrelevant to understanding maturity of personality and of faith, there are some parallels here between the Piagetian stage and psychoanalytic understanding of the same age. Child analysts observe that a child needs to develop gradually towards the differentiation of self and others, and needs to learn the relationship between internal experience and external reality. All of this has bearing on some types of religious thinking. For example, the distorted 'messianic type' of belief in which a person believes himself to be God shows confusion between self and the other. Rare though this extreme type of omnipotent thinking (and disturbed mental state) might be, narcissistic faith (concern for oneself and personal salvation more than concern for others) is more common, and is a forerunner of the type of magical thinking which is seen in more simplistic religious views.

In the intuitive stage isolated features of a problem are seen, with attention being paid to one aspect but other features being missed. The child cannot see that a partial solution might also give rise to new problems. In religious thinking this stage is seen in fairy-tale type of religion, where God, for instance, is seen as a king, larger than life, but in the manner of a fairy story, alongside dragons and other mythical creatures. In religious 'solutions' to questions an answer may give rise to other important questions which the child (or even the adult) cannot see as relevant. Mythology is a feature of the type of explanations that accompany this stage.

The stage of concrete thinking sees a major breakthrough, with systematic thought and the holding together of two or more aspects of a situation. It is, however, still difficult in this type of thinking to generalize or to think outside one's own experience. In religious thinking this is a more realistic stage, with God, for instance, seen as a father, and as much more like a human figure. Explanations of mystifying experiences are often a combination of the natural, the supernatural and the artificial.

The final stage of the development of thinking leads to the ability to think hypothetically, to form propositions, and to test them out in thought and not just in action. Symbolic and abstract terms can be conceptualized. One researcher calls this the 'individualistic stage'.[24] From this stage onwards interpretations of religious faith vary enormously from the conventional to the mystical, but natural explanations are much more readily understood, without having to have recourse to the supernatural.

Although I have illustrated Piaget with examples of religious thinking, it has been suggested that 'the entire religious development of the child has a much slower tempo than the development of any other field of his experience.'[25] This statement is of the highest importance in attempting to integrate the stages of cognitive development with the stages of personality development previously outlined. Faith is a much more difficult area for explanation than any other area, because it relies on abstract concepts, upon internal more than upon external experience, and on thinking and feeling more than upon the other senses. No wonder, then, that religious thinking in many adults has not moved far beyond the intuitive or concrete, even when in other areas of thought and experience those same people are able to work with the most complex abstract ideas. Furthermore, this slow tempo of development in the religious field means that the chronological ages, which have acted to this point in my account as guides, cease to have much meaning. One of the complications that is not immediately apparent in the diagrams I introduce from this point onwards is that religious and moral maturity tends to lag behind the parallel psycho-social and cognitive stages, so that – even though there are common features that lead to their vertical alignment – in practice the horizontal models develop at different speeds.

The research into religious thinking that emerged from Piaget's initial work finds parallels in the theologian Paul Tillich, who has described three types of world-view, Worlds A, B and C. World-view A consists of a natural first stage of literalism, found in primitive religion as well as in childhood, where the mythical is taken literally. In one sense in this stage there are no myths, because they are not recognized as such. They are the truth: the world was made in six 24-hour days, which can be 'dated' historically. A person with World-view A feels safe and secure, and often unquestioning of their faith.

If and when this questioning occurs, World-view A becomes untenable. People then move to World-view B, some for a short time, some for ever. Tillich calls this a stage of 'conscious literalism'. The person in the stage of conscious literalism needs external authority (normally of the Church or the Bible) to supply answers to troubling questions. Such authority often represses the doubts by providing means of enabling literal explanations to be retained. Creation's six days, for example, are now explained as geological eras. For the time being questions are answered.

Where questioning persists, or the answers provided do not satisfy, Tillich suggests people move to World-view C, which he calls 'broken myth'. Here natural explanations can be accepted, but without losing sight of the value of the myth, as now pointing beyond necessary scientific and rational explanations to ultimate concerns. 'Myth addresses the nature of the ultimate while geology attends to that which is less than ultimate, namely, the age of the earth.'[26] World-view C is not without its anxiety, because myths and symbols do not provide certain answers. Doubts are not resolved by the magic explanations of literalism or by the sacred authority of conscious literalism. Faith and courage (two of Tillich's key words) conquer doubt, but do not eliminate it.

While Tillich's three world-views can be placed, albeit somewhat arbitrarily, within the chart which I have been building up throughout this chapter, I think myself that Tillich made a huge jump when he moved from World B to World C. It is not difficult, for instance, to think of people who no longer accept symbols literally, and who are not content with the explanations of sacred authority, but who have no conception that myth and symbol can point to ultimate concerns. The World C person has moved a long way towards mature faith, but appears to have jumped at least one step along the way. For this reason I place a question-mark between World-views B and C, pushing the latter well into the second half of life. I doubt if World-view C appears with much frequency before mid-life, and I do not know how widespread it is even then. Fowler's work, which helps to fill some of the gaps between World B and World C, seems to suggest that symbols and myths are not used in this creative but non-literal way until (his) Stage 5, and that fewer people reach this stage.

JUNG	Youth First half of life (Establishing)	Mid-life	Old Age
		Second half of life (Individuation)	
LEVINSON	Early Adulthood	Mid Adulthood	Late Adulthood
	Transition	Transition	
ERIKSON	Young Adulthood Intimacy *vs* Isolation	Mid Adulthood Generativity/Creativity *vs* Stagnation	Maturity Integrity *vs* Despair
TILLICH	?	World-view C Broken Myth and Use of Symbols	

Figure 7: Tillich's World-view C

Before looking at Fowler's stages, it is interesting to note that, in a book whose title is reminiscent of developmental themes (*Life Lines*[27]), Cupitt sets out his own map of theological approaches to questions about the meaning of life. I shall refer in later chapters to some of his stages of theological thinking, since 'mythical realism' and 'doctrinal realism' (to give two examples) fit in well, as two types of institutional religion, with World-views A and B. However, it is necessary to observe that Cupitt does not propose a single linear track in his model, but a type of Metro map with a web of interconnected lines. His diagram and the particular technical terms he uses cannot be neatly integrated into the chart which I am developing here, but his study acts as a reminder that the 'sacred authority' which Tillich's World-view B type uses is not in fact static in its own interpretation. I suspect that what distinguishes a World-view B person is not a particular interpretation of scripture or tradition, but the use he or she makes of sacred authority, to defend against personal anxiety and questioning.

Fowler's Model of Faith Development

Some of the most fascinating research that has been done on the relationship between psychological development and faith and religion has appeared since the mid-1970s in the work of James Fowler and his colleagues.[28] While this work is still being critically evaluated and refined, the pastoral care of growing persons cannot ignore the stages of faith which he proposes. Fowler originally drew upon the theories of Piaget, Erikson and Kohlberg, the first two of whom I have already included in this chapter, and the third of whom I describe shortly. Fowler and his team conducted long interviews with people of all ages, and from the data collected he has set out seven stages of faith, numbered from 0 to 6. He has himself integrated these stages with the Erikson model, and in various writings has drawn different diagrams to show the parallels. Faith development moves at such diverse rates in individual people that any diagrammatic representation tends to oversimplify, but I have adapted one of his charts[29] for inclusion in my own, in attempt to show the way in which Fowler's work on faith and Kohlberg's work on moral development fit into other aspects of personal growth and maturity. However, I have marked the stages with broken lines to suggest the need in practice to keep these boundaries flexible, less tied to chronological age than is psycho-social development.

I use Fowler's descriptions of these stages extensively in the following chapters, making it unnecessary at this point to explain them in more detail, although the reader may find it valuable at later points to refer back to Figure 8.

Kohlberg and Moral Development

Although Kohlberg's research into the development of moral thinking and attitudes antedates Fowler's research into faith development, the latter's publications have given rise to further work by Kohlberg on the relationship between moral and faith development, and to the question of the significance of faith in moral attitudes. Fowler's stage 6 encouraged Kohlberg to develop the latter's earlier speculation about a further 'stage' of moral development, over and above the six stages which are supported by the data from his research.[30]

Kohlberg outlined six stages of moral development, divided into three levels of judgement, each level consisting of two distinct stages. The basis of moral judgement in each of the three levels is pre-conventional, conventional and self-

JUNG	Childhood		Youth			Mid-life		Old Age
	First half of life (Establishing)					Second half of life (Individuation)		
LEVINSON	Childhood and Adolescence		Transition	Early Adulthood	Transition	Mid Adulthood	Transition	Late Adulthood
FREUD	Oral	Anal	Genital	Latency	Adolescence			
ERIKSON	Trust *vs* Mistrust	Autonomy *vs* Shame	Initiative *vs* Guilt	Industry *vs* Inferiority	Identity *vs* Confusion	Young Adulthood Intimacy *vs* Isolation	Mid Adulthood Generativity/Creativity *vs* Stagnation	Maturity Integrity *vs* Despair
PIAGET	sensori-motor intelligence	intuitive thinking	concrete thinking	abstract thinking				
TILLICH	World-view A pre-conscious literalism	World-view B conscious literalism	?	World-view C Broken Myth and Use of Symbols				
FOWLER	O. Primal Faith	1. Intuitive–Projective Faith	2. Mythic–Literal Faith	3. Synthetic–Conventional Faith	4. Individuative–Reflective Faith	5. Conjunctive Faith	'6. Universalizing Faith'	
KOHLBERG'S *Bases for Morality*	1. Fear	2. Self-interest	3. Conformity	4. Social Order	5. Rights of others	6. Universal Principles	'Stage 7'	
	(pre-conventional)		(conventional)		(self-accepted)			

Figure 8: Completing the chart with Fowler's stages of Faith Development and Kohlberg's stages of Moral Development

accepted moral principles. The six stages can be briefly described by indicating the motivation for moral thinking and action present in each, and the equivalent religious thinking (where it is present) that follows from each position. Thus, in the first stage, the motive behind moral decisions is fear of superior powers such as parents or God, and the need to protect oneself against punishment. God is therefore experienced as punisher or rewarder. The second stage (also part of the pre-conventional level) involves a different selfish motive of satisfying one's own needs through 'bargaining' with others. 'I'll scratch your back if you'll scratch mine' is Kohlberg's way of summarizing this stage, with the religious equivalent being, 'You be good to God and he'll be good to you.'[31]

The third and fourth stages form the conventional level of moral judgement. In the third, moral decisions are based on a desire to conform to the expectations of the community, and on doing good to gain approval and please other people. Although in the Freudian/Erikson model conformity to parental 'rules' and 'will' is part of the anal stage (with issues of authority and autonomy to the fore) the placing of this Kohlberg stage on a parallel with the Freudian stage called 'latency' (Figure 8) concurs with children going to school, meeting for the first time the socialization process, and hence beginning to come up against the rules and pressures that lead, in most children, to social conformity. Religious reasoning in the third Kohlberg stage sees God as ideally good, and the protector of goodness, with common images of him as a personal deity, a friend or a caring shepherd. The fourth stage is one of doing one's duty, respecting authority, and of working to maintain the social order for its own sake. It does not at first sit neatly below adolescence, which is stereotypically anti-authority. But in fact adolescence is equally a time in which many young people move from dependence upon authority to respect for it, and from periods of anarchic thinking to an understanding of what society expects of them. If our image of adolescence is one of rebellion, I have often heard the experience of adulthood described by people in their twenties as having had to sell out to the system.

Religious thinking linked to this fourth stage sees God as being bound by his own laws, and as the ultimate ground of order. God may be conceptualized in more abstract terms such as 'the supreme being' or 'the cosmic force'. Where religious thinking is present it often expresses reverence for God's order and moral law.

The fifth and six stages comprise the third level, which is based more upon self-accepted principles than upon conventional rules. Stage 5 is represented by moral thinking which respects the rights of others, and which upholds society's duty not to violate the rights of the individual. In this stage religious reasoning presents God and human beings as mutually involved in creating a community in which dignity and freedom is encouraged. The sixth stage is one of much greater orientation towards conscience, over and above socially ordained rules, with recognition that moral responsibility sometimes means disobeying unjust laws.

Fowler has drawn up his own plan which fits Kohlberg's stages alongside his own, and Kohlberg clearly sees his six stages of moral and religious reasoning as parallel to Fowler's stages 1 to 6.[32] I place Kohlberg's stages in slightly different positions, where I think they also fit well with some of Erikson's Eight Ages. My own placing follows Kohlberg's view that moral development often precedes faith development. His numbered stages therefore anticipate Fowler's. By looking vertically through the chart, it becomes clear that the Kohlberg stages generally reflect the same issues as both the Erikson ages and the Fowler stages of faith. For example, the first stage of moral thinking, based on fear of superiors, overlaps with the fear of parental figures in Erikson's second 'authority' stage. Conformity to conventions fits in well with pre-adolescence. Similarly, respect for the rights of the others seems to fit well with the need for acceptance of separateness and differences when entering into a close relationship, and in subsequent parenthood, where respect for the 'otherness' of children is an essential part of helping them to develop as individuals, and not as parental clones. Erikson, Jung, Fowler and Kohlberg each stress in their final stages a sense of coming together and of wholeness, and of being one with the cosmos.

An explanation is necessary of 'stage 7' in the Kohlberg part of the chart. Kohlberg found it difficult to stop at the sixth stage, because he felt that some kind of religious reason is required to support the sixth stage of belief in principles. The question at that stage of 'Why be moral?' need no longer be answered by self-interest or the need to conform. It appears to involve questions about meaning. 'Ultimate moral maturity requires a mature solution to the question of the meaning of life.'[33] It is for this reason that Kohlberg suggests a somewhat imprecise 'stage 7', nearly always enclosed in inverted commas, to show that it is more a metaphor than an actual stage. Since I argue in chapter 7, that Fowler's stage 6, 'Universalizing Faith', is not a definite stage of development, the reader will notice that I have chosen to place it too in inverted commas.

Kohlberg believes that 'stage 7' arises out of the despair that comes from the realization of one's finiteness, and of the meaninglessness of the finite compared to the infinite. There is clearly a link here to Tillich's analysis of anxiety as arising out of the recognition of death and despair, and Tillich's description of courage (one of the cardinal moral virtues) as the affirmation of the power of life over death.[34]

'Stage 7' comes out of the resolution of despair. It represents a state of mind in which there is a sense of being part of the whole of life, identified with the cosmic, infinite perspective itself. Kohlberg contrasts such a view with his stage 6 perspective which he calls 'universal humanistic'. In Judaeo-Christian terms 'stage 7' is expressed as a sense of union with God, but the faith involved need not be of this order. Kohlberg deliberately cites the Roman emperor Marcus Aurelius as an example of 'stage 7', although he adds a further example of a Quaker woman whose religious orientation was a blend of Eastern and Western mysticism.

Although 'stage 7' is used by Kohlberg as a metaphor rather than as a definite stage, it is the only one of the stages he describes where religious thinking comes first. In the main six stages he claims that attainment of a particular moral stance is necessary for the equivalent religious stage to be reached. This suggests that (with the exception of 'stage 7') people do not develop a specific moral attitude from their religious faith (as Christians tend to believe), but rather that their religious thinking develops from their moral position. If Kohlberg is correct (or indeed only partially correct), such a hypothesis has the effect of questioning the way in which much preaching and teaching insists on starting with theological ideas and images, and using them to promote changes in moral thinking and action: 'God loves you, therefore love one another.' In the light of Kohlberg, it is worth asking whether such an admonition makes any sense unless a person has already reached the stage of loving others – in which case, of course, it does not need to be said. However, for the development of a mature faith, it may be that starting from moral values and actions, or (as I suggested at the end of the last chapter) from human relationships, is more productive than using the 'power' of sacred texts or doctrines. There is, of course, nothing new in this, since Jesus himself taught by parables, pointing out, from human stories, how these situations reflected the nature of God. A brief example of this technique is seen in the Sermon on the Mount: 'If you . . . know how to give your children what is good for them, how much more will your heavenly Father give good things to those who ask him!'[35]

That religious belief should follow other aspects of personality development is also borne out by the research (to which I refer in chapter 4) on the influence of early upbringing on views and images of God. From all sides it appears that the movement towards the fullness of Christ cannot be understood in isolation from the rest of life. Since the fullness of Christ is rooted in the Incarnation, it is extremely doubtful whether Christian maturity should ever be separated from the growth of the whole person. Pastoral care which aims at assisting the maturational process cannot use religious convictions and spirituality in isolation, but needs to learn from the models which I have briefly outlined in this chapter, and which form the basis for later chapters. However, it is also necessary to use models discriminately, and in the next chapter I turn to a few cautions about the way a pastor interprets these different views about development and growth.

1. Piaget's theories are set out thoroughly, with some of the questions raised by them, in J. L. Phillips, *The Origins of Intellect* (USA, W. H. Freeman, 1975).
2. R. Goldman, *Religious Thinking from Childhood to Adolescence* (Routledge and Kegan Paul 1964).
3. J. W. Fowler, *Stages of Faith: the Psychology of Human Development and the Quest for Meaning* (San Francisco, Harper and Row, 1981).
4. See chapter 1, note 1.
5. Frieda Fordham, *An Introduction to Jung's Psychology* (Penguin 1966), pp. 78–9.
6. ibid., p. 78.
7. A. Samuels, *Jung and the Post-Jungians* (Routledge and Kegan Paul 1985), ch. 5.
8. Fordham, op. cit., p. 79.
9. D. Levinson, *et al.*, *The Seasons of a Man's Life* (New York, Knopf, 1978). See also J. W. Fowler, *Becoming Adult, Becoming Christian* (San Francisco, Harper and Row, 1984), pp. 30–7.
10. Levinson, op. cit., p. 6–7.
11. Fowler, *Becoming Adult*, p. 33.
12. Naomi Golan, *Passing Through Transitions* (London, Collier Macmillan, 1981).
13. M. Jacobs, *The Presenting Past* (Open University Press 1986). I now prefer the longer and more complete description of GS included in this text to the one in my earlier book.
14. H. Faber, *Psychology of Religion* (SCM Press 1976).
15. Sallie McFague, *Models of God* (Fortress Press and SCM Press 1987).
16. E. Erikson, *Childhood and Society* (Penguin 1965), ch. 8.
17. For the complete list see Jacobs, *The Presenting Past*, p. xiii.
18. E. Erikson, *Young Man Luther* (Faber 1959); *Gandhi's Truth* (New York, W. W. Norton, 1969).
19. See, for example, R. L. Randall, 'Stages in the Role Cycle of Pastoral Counseling' (*The Journal of Pastoral Care*, XXXVI, 2, 1982, pp. 93–104).
20. D. Capps, *Life Cycle Theory and Pastoral Care* (Fortress Press 1983). For the application of life-cycle theory to pastoral counselling issues see also D. Capps, *Pastoral Care: a Thematic Approach* (Philadelphia, Westminster Press, 1969).
21. S. Freud, *Obsessive Actions and Religious Practices* in Pelican Freud Library, vol. 13 (Penguin 1985), pp. 31–41.
22. Capps, op. cit., p. 61.
23. See also H. P. V. Renner, 'The Use of Ritual in Pastoral Care'

(*The Journal of Pastoral Care*, xxxiii, 3, 1979, pp. 164–74). Renner draws upon Erikson's view of the basic roots of ritualization as coming from relationships between people.

24. Harms, in Goldman, op. cit., pp. 24–5.
25. Goldman, op. cit., p. 25.
26. W. E. Baldridge and J. J. Gleason, 'A Theological Framework for Pastoral Care' (*The Journal of Pastoral Care*, xxxii, 4, 1978, pp. 232–8). I draw this explanation of Tillich's world-views from this article, which can also be found in an abbreviated form in M. Jacobs, *Faith or Fear* (Darton Longman and Todd 1987). Tillich's world-views can be found in his *Dynamics of Faith* (New York, Harper, 1957).
27. D. Cupitt, *Life Lines* (SCM Press 1986).
28. J. W. Fowler, *Stages of Faith – the Psychology of Human Development and the Quest for Meaning* (San Francisco, Harper and Row, 1981); *Becoming Adult, Becoming Christian* (San Francisco, Harper and Row, 1984); *Faith Development and Pastoral Care* (Fortress Press 1987).
29. Fowler, *Stages of Faith*, p. 113.
30. L. Kohlberg, *The Philosophy of Moral Development* (San Francisco, Harper and Row, 1981).
31. ibid., p. 341. I draw upon this section of Kohlberg's book in the description of his moral stages.
32. ibid., p. 334.
33. L. Kohlberg, 'Education, Moral Development and Faith' (*Journal of Moral Education*, iv, 1, p. 14).
34. P. Tillich, *The Courage to Be* (Nisbet 1952).
35. Matt. 7:10–11.

3

Cautions

In describing the different models that help chart human development in its various aspects – cognitive, emotional, religious and moral – I have expressed reservations about taking the models too literally. I turn now to look at some of these cautionary aspects, aware that models are designed to assist understanding, but not to dictate it. They have the same value as charts and maps, giving sufficient guidance to the paths of development, but inevitably limited to one dimension. In reality human development is multi-dimensional, something which the use of models must always reflect.

Against Narrow Thinking

The necessity of making a model intelligible leads in the majority of diagrams to a linear representation, as if development takes a single path, passing through definite stages in a pre-determined order. The question of determinism or predestination is as much a psychological question as it is a philosophical or theological one. Although general directions are predictable, the study of human development always has to allow room for individual variations, which arise from the large number of variables which influence any one person's life.

Cupitt, as noted earlier, adopts a Metro map rather than a single route, with tracks moving from one 'line' to another at different points,[1] but this is unusual. Fowler indicates that the ages spanned by most of his stages of faith have blurred edges. Although none of the models represented insists on a rigidly linear scheme, there is nevertheless a temptation to link stages to ages, and to see each stage as being complete in itself. Transitional periods apart, it is necessary to interpret the models as representing a dynamic movement, and not as static. Most people pass to and fro between the different stages at various points in their lives, depending upon external circumstances and individual internal responses.

Some models, such as Kohlberg's moral stages and Fowler's faith stages, have to be understood as representing a journey which many people do not complete, even in the course of a lifetime. This does not make them any less respected as persons (see the caution against narrow ambition below). Other models, such as Erikson's, cover the different stages of most people's lives, but indicate the various resolutions which arise in each stage, sometimes satisfactory, sometimes less so. In most models people reach a particular stage only by passing through the preceding ones: they do not, for instance, jump from Level One in Kohlberg's scheme to Level Three, and then back to Level Two. But if the order is predictable, this does not rule out an important qualification in looking at any of the models, that at times people temporarily 'regress' (in psychoanalytic jargon) to earlier stages.

At the same time I want to go further and suggest the possibility that at different stages of development not only are features of earlier stages still present, but also that later stages are prefigured. There are particular links between first and last stages in both Erikson and Fowler, where the sense of being part of the universal in the last stage is prefigured in the awareness of and wish for continuing unity with the maternal figure in the first stage.

While at first sight Erikson's Eight Ages, in his original diagram, look like an ascending staircase, Capps makes it clear that Erikson also uses a cyclical image of development in two respects. Firstly he suggests that the different generations interlock like cogwheels, so that movement in one generation is an integral part of movement in the next: thus adults develop as parents at the same time as their children grow through childhood. A second image that Erikson employs is that of a series of concentric circles, where the boundaries of an individual's relationships expand as life progresses, from interaction with the maternal figure, through relating to both parents, to the whole family, to school friends and the wider peer group, to close relationships outside the family, to relationships at work and in society, and finally to identification with the universal.[2] I have myself tried to combine these different images of straight ascent and the circle by showing that Erikson's model of human development can best be understood through the analogy of a spiral staircase, which has eight treads to each complete turn of its ascent. Each of the major issues in human development (the eight 'conflicts' between strengths and weaknesses in Figures 4 and 5) appear in some form at every stage of life (each circular flight). At the same time each of the issues forms a vertical column passing through the Eight Ages. So trust, for example, is not just the issue of stage 1, but takes a different form, and has to be renegotiated during the whole of life.[3]

A rather different approach to personality, which deserves mention since it has caught the attention of some church educators and pastors, is the Myers-Briggs Type Indicator.[4] This is not a linear model at all, but rather 'places' people, as a result of an easily administered paper test, in one of sixteen different temperaments. These temperaments are partly based upon Jung's description of four psychological types, the sensing, thinking, intuitive and feeling person, together with other characteristics such as extraversion, introversion, judging and perceiving. Certain characteristics tend to predominate in any one individual. Scoring of the test results in a personal profile, which might be read like a newspaper horoscope (inasmuch as it gives plenty of scope for a person to see what they want to see about themselves) were it not for the number of details listed. The profile is careful to avoid approval or disapproval of the many characteristics that are ascribed to the test subject. Nevertheless, as a person reads his or her own self description, an individual may feel that he or she has particular personal strengths, as well as particular personal weaknesses. As in Jungian psychology itself, the strengthening of the weaker parts of the self comes through looking to one's 'shadow side'. The 'thinking' person will benefit from accepting more of his or her 'feeling', the extravert more of his or her introversion, and so on.

Myers-Briggs is a useful tool for helping people to reflect

more deeply upon themselves with a certain degree of objectivity. It stands as a reminder that there are built-in influences on the way individuals develop throughout life, in the particular bias of their temperament or psychological type. Inasmuch as the test can be taken at different stages, it might demonstrate how much, or how little, a person has 'changed'. It does not, however, seek to explain what makes a person the type they are, nor does it suggest a direction in which a person might move. It is, as it were, a fingerprint of a person rather than a journal of their development. Myers-Briggs tells us little about maturity itself, except in what it takes from the Jungian individuation process, where neglected aspects of the personality are encouraged to develop and play a fuller part in the whole person. Yet the test certainly provides another dimension (that of temperament), which, taken together with the other dimensions that I introduce in this chapter, helps qualify and expand the inevitably limited vision that comes from the models described in the last chapter.

The analogy I have been using, that of the chart or map, becomes more complete if we take into account the temperament of the map-reader and walker, as well as the true nature of a cross country ramble. When planning a route across country, a walker often starts by drawing a straight line from start to finish, in order to plan a rough route to the point of destination. Having drawn such a line, a route needs to be planned which stays with footpaths and bridleways, which skirts lakes and impenetrable woods, and which finds the best place to cross rivers. With what enthusiasm the walker turns plan into action, or stays with the plan, depends to some extent upon the temperament of the walker, and to some extent on the actual nature of the terrain he or she discovers. Having started the walk, the rambler may find it necessary to backtrack occasionally when an unmapped obstacle appears, such as a ripe field of corn, or a missing bridge. In the end the walker's route goes back and forth, while at the same time progressing towards the destination. Various temperaments may mean that different satisfactions arise for different people in the taking and completion of the walk. As long as human development is perceived in this realistic way, the charts provide a valuable, but far from perfect, perspective.

Against Narrow Ambition

There is a further difficulty with most models, which is not the fault of the model, but more part of the psychology of the person employing it. Whether the model is one-dimensional or multi-faceted, it is tempting to use it as yardstick to measure maturity, in the same way as some people use intelligence tests in the hope of placing themselves in a special, superior category. While maturity is a goal worth seeking, and the path towards it a direction worth taking, it can never be an aim that has to be achieved at all costs, like another school prize or further academic qualification. Erikson warns against the 'success ideology which can so dangerously pervade our private and public daydreams'.[5] The competitive spirit, which sometimes assists development, can also ruin it, when parents (and through them their children) measure personal worth through standards of physical, financial and intellectual achievement, from the baby who walks before others of its age, to the status that is imagined to come from academic or sporting success, from material wealth, or from position in society. Erikson's work, like that of other child psychologists, can unfortunately, and mistakenly, lead to people measuring themselves against others, and against notional norms.

To use models of human development in this way is to distort them, much as spiritual exercises will be distorted if used in an effort to become a saint. Alternatively, such models can be used as sticks to beat oneself with, for failing to reach supposed standards of growth and maturity. Such a misuse of models is likely to feature strongly amongst religious people, who feel guilty when they do not achieve the high standards set by their faith (or more accurately by themselves). Achieving the right balance is difficult, because most of us would like to be better people, to be more mature and to find greater fulfilment. But to strive too conscientiously towards that end is often to create a rod for one's own back, and at worst to be forced into the very antithesis of maturity. There is a particular type of religion, which is not untypical, that bears considerable resemblance to the unresolved anal stage of development. In such religious thinking and behaviour there is an obsession with one's performance as a Christian, a legalistic emphasis on doing things in the correct way and in the proper order. Other more positive features of that stage of life are missing. Producing results predominates over relaxed enjoyment of play, of work and of simply being. If we are not to fall into that trap, it is important to recognize that the stages which the models suggest are descriptions of where people may be, not commands to be somewhere different. If, on the cross country ramble, the walker is continuously anxious to reach the next landmark, the present scene will neither be enjoyed nor appreciated. The walk becomes a race against time, against nature, and against oneself. No amount of extra effort will get the walker any quicker to the destination. Desperate striving to reach into the future is as unhelpful and as stultifying as mournful looking back over the shoulder to what has been left behind in the past.

An obsessional need to achieve maturity has no place in a positive view of personal development, whether in terms of relationships to others or in respect of attitudes to faith. A truly dynamic view of people allows for flexibility and fluidity. It draws upon models, but does not rigidly adhere to them. The models themselves describe developmental aspects, and not persons as such. One person may show a very simple faith which would not suit another more questioning individual. Yet the one who has simple faith might have a wider moral sense in Kohlberg's terms, and be more complete in emotional development in Erikson's terms, than the questioning individual whose faith is, on the Fowler scheme, at a higher stage of development. The models can, I believe, help a pastor to recognize the different stages towards wholeness at which people are, and at the right time to assist those people as they move from one stage to another. It is often transitional periods that are the hardest to endure, since they frequently involve a shaking up of cherished values, beliefs and attitudes. The models might also help the pastor find where he or she is. But in all this I would not wish to write anything which makes my readers worry if they appear to have taken a different route, if they are somewhere other than they had anticipated, or even back at a point they thought they had left behind some years before. There is value in the ebb and flow, in moving in and out of stages, in looking for the destination, but always prepared for it to be over the hill or even far away. And it is essential (though ironically of course this only comes with a certain degree of maturity) that we do not think ourselves better or worse depending on how near we reach our destination.

A particularly useful example of this much less competitive way of understanding ourselves is seen in Hemenway's description of four faith frameworks.[6] She provides a necessary corrective to the temptation to achieve which the progressive element in the more linear models encourages. Hemenway describes four types of theological and faith outlook. The first is a theology which emphasizes the Fall, sin, evil, alienation and judgement. Rules feature strongly in this type of religion. The second is a theology which emphasizes the good news of redemption, and the triumph of good over evil. Christology, atonement, evangelism, and the strong emphasis on faith are all features of this framework. The third is typified by an emphasis on relationship, on the covenant relationship throughout history between God and Israel and God and the Church. There is more interest in the Holy Spirit as sustaining, than in the more charismatic view of the second model. The struggle between good and evil goes on still, and there is more sense of a developmental and historical unfolding of salvation. The last framework emphasizes the unity in creation, the oneness between the 'I am' and 'we are'; the acceptance of death as part of life, and not as a defeat. There is more ecological and radical concern associated with this outlook than with the others. The theological stress is on Creation and the Creator. The main personal features of this outlook include hope, responsibility for and participation in life and the natural order, and the realization of wholeness and fullness of being.

These valuable analyses of personal attitudes and theological emphases have certain resemblances to some stages in the models considered so far, and will be echoed in the more detailed descriptions that follow this chapter. The first framework has similar features to religion based on rules and fear.

The second with its interest in personal salvation, contains aspects which remind me of the concern for self seen in Kohlberg's moral stage 3 of self-interest, yet it also has signs of a youthful, energetic adolescence in its tendency to enthusiasm. The third shares in some respects the sense of community and concern for social order that features in Kohlberg's moral stage 4. Hemenway also indicates that this framework has much in common with the developmental approach as a whole, and mentions in that context Fowler, Erikson and Piaget. The fourth framework has many resemblances to the universalizing faith and universal principles in Fowler and Kohlberg respectively, and in its attitude towards death as the completion of life, there is much in common with Erikson's eighth age, where integrity and wholeness also feature strongly.

Yet none of her frameworks fit precisely into the developmental models. A feature here, an emphasis there, a parallel from one stage and yet a contradiction in another – all these are apparent if we try to line her faith frameworks up with any of the columns on the chart of development. This underlines her own point, that the four frameworks are not 'developmental in nature, so that a person moves 'back' towards No. 1 and 'forward' to No. 4. Thinking in this way would imply a value judgement that some stages are more 'healthy' than others.[7] She emphasizes that we all move back and forth between these different frameworks, depending to some extent upon mood. She links theological outlook to psychological feeling. Hemenway says that the frameworks have to be used multi-dimensionally, and she too suggests they can be seen as four strands that spiral together. Development and growth involve looking for all four strands within oneself, and gradually deciding which strands need to be developed, which discarded and which affirmed.

Hemenway's approach, which urges use of all aspects of her model in understanding personal and faith development, is one which I too want to underline, in the hope that the reader can draw discriminately but also widely upon the whole chart of development in Figure 8, rather than look for identification with one set of stages. It is also important to emphasize that at whatever stage of development a person is, each has the same worth and the same potential for 'holiness', within the frame of reference which each person has. This acceptance of the present stage of the individual, as well as the hope of further growth and development, underpins both the psychotherapeutic and the pastoral outlooks.

Against Narrow Labelling

In addition to the danger of looking to models to provide a personal sense of the achievement of progress, models can also be used to stereotype and label others. Hemenway admits that her own frameworks are over-simplified and somewhat stereotypical, and insists that they have to be used creatively, as jumping-off points to playing with ideas and perceptions.[8] There is a temptation to use categories and concepts to caricature other people, especially where there is antipathy between differing groups. On the other hand, there is a religious concept of 'naming', which is opposed to the pejorative use of labelling. Naming is used in contexts where there is the forging (sometimes after a struggle) of close, intimate and loving relationships between people.[9] Models, and the jargon that inevitably accompanies them, can be used in pastoral care to comprehend people better, and therefore to assist the process of forging relationships which are based upon understanding as well as love.

There is a further danger in using terms as labels, that we can stereotype people without recognizing the uniqueness of each individual. I have already stressed this important qualification. In addition, a caution is necessary about treating the development of men and women (and indeed people of different cultures) as identical. It was Freud who first suggested that psychological development takes different paths when boys and girls are about four or five years old. In fact the divergence may come earlier, since evidence suggests different attitudes in mothers towards baby sons and daughters, and that this early relationship influences the different attitudes seen in boys or girls, as well as men and women, both to themselves and to others.[10] Even though Freud was himself doubtful of his ability to understand women, both he and many other male psychologists and therapists have often written as if male and female development were identical.

The models already outlined have all been designed by men, from interpretations which they, as men, have given to research data from men and women. This does not of itself invalidate their work but it does call for more caution about development necessarily being the same in all respects. Naomi Golan[11] makes it clear that the separate decades of adult life give rise to different issues for men and for women. Levinson followed his book *Seasons of a Man's Life* with research into the seasons of women's lives. Carol Gilligan has seriously questioned Kohlberg's emphasis on justice as a measure of moral development, and has herself placed greater emphasis, especially in women, on connectedness and relationships.[12]

Gilligan, one of Kohlberg's colleagues, was concerned that most women were rarely placed in moral development stage 4, but mainly in stage 3. It appeared that women were less developed in their moral thinking than men. She went back to the research and discovered that women tended to approach the moral questions which were used in the interviews in different ways. They were less concerned with rules, and more with relationships, with where actions might lead, and with the history that lay behind the moral dilemmas. This sense of connectedness and responsibility seemed to be a feature in women, which Gilligan distinguished from the ethics of duty which predominated in men. She also found parallels for her findings in psychoanalytic writings on the gender differences in the mother–baby relationship.

Gilligan's work shows how careful we need to be about identifying men and women, although it also reminds us that we cannot stereotype all men as the same, or all women as the same. Could there be significant differences in what constitutes maturity in men and in women? Although Kohlberg originally provided only one example of 'stage 7' moral thinking, Marcus Aurelius, and the importance to him of justice as part of natural law, in his later work he seems to have taken account of Gilligan's qualifications, including as a further and different example a Quaker woman, in whom *agape* was the main evidence of her 'stage 7' thinking and motivation.

Nevertheless as the final stages of maturity are approached, what is integral to them, in whatever scheme we use, is a developing sense of wholeness and of unity with others and with the universe. Maturity involves bringing together different aspects of personality, some of which might have been undeveloped in earlier life. The Jungian goal of individuation involves people embracing these less developed sides of themselves, men accepting their 'feminine' side, and women their 'masculine' side. Psychological studies of gender suggest many of the stereotypes of men and women arise from the process of socialization, and need to be re-examined, so that men allow themselves to become more sensitive to others and the world about them, and women more assertive of their rights of independence. Freud did not believe that terms to describe differences in psychological characteristics in men and women served any useful purpose.[13]

From all sides there appears confirmation for regarding maturity as a stage where the apparently 'masculine' and apparently 'feminine' come together, to form the wholeness which Paul describes in another (and rather more reductive) way when he writes that in Christ 'there is no such thing as . . . male and female'.[14] Fowler sums up Gilligan's work in a more inclusive way, as showing 'that moral maturity, for women and for men, means balancing responsibility and care with a keen sense of rights and justice, along with learning to deal with the inevitable tensions and ambiguities that this will involve. This may be an important dimension of the integration, in mature adulthood, of the masculine and the feminine modalities in our lives.'[15] Fullness of Christ involves embracing the image that 'Christ is all, and is in all'.[16]

Against Narrow Faith

The reader interested enough to follow thus far the parallels between personal faith and moral development, does not perhaps need to be warned that faith, as defined by any of the authors of the models described, is employed as an inclusive rather than an exclusive term. Inevitably, given my own background and training, I write from a Christian perspective, as the tradition which has informed my own understanding of faith. But I acknowledge, in common with those from whom I draw my own insights, that faith is a universal phenomenon, and cannot be confined to Christian creeds and experience. Fowler's definition of faith, which forms the basis for his study, is, as he admits himself, somewhat formal in its attempt to be comprehensive.[17] Kohlberg's summary of it is rather easier to use in this context: 'Fowler defines faith as people's orientation to the ultimate environment in terms of what they value as being most relevant and important to their entire lives.'[18] Faith therefore embraces, as one of Fowler's mentors wrote:

> The involvement of the Christian with God and with Christ and with the sacraments and with the moral imperatives and with the community; the involvement of the Hindu with caste and with the law of retributive justice and the *maya*-quality of this mundane world and with the vision of the final liberation; the involvement of the Buddhist with the image of the Buddha and with the moral law and with an institutionalized moral order and with the dream of a further shore beyond this sea of sorrow; the involvement of the primitive animist with the world perceived in poetic, if bizarre, vitality and responsiveness.[19]

And, we could add, faith is equally the meaning, or even the inability to give meaning (which in itself is, albeit negative, an expression of belief) that is present in the atheist, the agnostic or the unthinking bigot.

Such definitions of faith clearly include different aspects of Christian belief, and it is natural that in this context I should dwell almost exclusively upon that particular expression rather than upon any other. But an essential feature of the final stages of maturity in Fowler, Erikson, Jung and Kohlberg (and, in a curious way, as we shall see, in Freud's analysis of religion) is the universal dimension, so that even Christian faith moves in the direction of an openness to learning from alternative expressions, and from the symbols and images of other faiths. While it can never lose its particular appeal for the individual Christian, or for the society which has Christianity as its cultural bedrock, all those who describe maturity agree that the vision that comes from faith enlarges and embraces other ways of seeing. If maturity involves, on the part of the individual, a sense of oneness with the rest of creation and of being part of the whole, no less can be asked of an institutionalized faith as it too reaches towards a mature vision: the transcendent must, by definition, be larger than any religion.

By faith I also mean not just intellectual assent, and not just ways of thinking, but the experience of faith as well. Clearly an important part of faith is spirituality, which can perhaps be described as faith in action. My own studies have been in psychology rather than in spirituality, and others are much better placed to describe traditional and current ways of understanding the movement towards mature spiritual life. Yet spirituality is evidently so much part of the whole person that it cannot be divorced from this study. I attempt to include aspects of it, as faith in action, in the chapters that follow, culminating in what appear to be close links between spirituality and maturity in the last chapter. Since writers on the spiritual life also use images of the journey, of the ascending ladder, and of passing through the rooms of an interior castle to innermost being,[20] developmental sequences are clearly as important to them as they are to the psychologists who tend to inform my thinking.

A More Open Way

If the last chapter appeared to set up the value of various current models of development, this one may appear to have knocked them down again. My concern for relatively straightforward models has to be balanced by an acknowledgement of the limitations they share with other metaphors even though, like other symbols and signs, they can also point us towards new ways of understanding. I am more concerned with the development of attitudes than with being tied too firmly down to actual ages or to strict stages. While the last chapter resulted in a chart which maps out a number of complementary paths through the complex patterns of development, I intend from this point to concentrate upon four aspects of the movement towards maturity, symbolized in the image 'the fullness of Christ'. Conveniently, by combining pairs of the Fowler stages with Faber's oral, anal and genital religion, I can link these phases with my own preference for seeing three or four major sets of themes as weaving their way through all life's stages.

The fluid and dynamic nature of personal development, to which a printed chart can scarcely do justice, requires us to make links between different stages, and various viewpoints. Thus, by connecting Fowler's Stages of Faith 0 and 1 with the Freud/Faber/Erikson views of early infancy and oral religion, there is much in common with what can be called 'oral stage' themes – trust, dependency, phantasy, etc. These I examine in chapter 4 – 'Origins'. Fowler's stages 2 and 3 come together with a psychoanalytic understanding of the anal stage and of anal religion, and tie in with themes of authority and autonomy, rules and conformity. These I look at in chapter 5 – 'Conventions'. The Fowler stages 4 and 5, together with Freud/Faber/Erikson views on the development of a distinct identity, come together with 'genital stage' themes such as gender, sexuality, social relations, co-operation, and competition. Chapter 6 – 'Diversities' – looks at these aspects, and at the way in which the models converge as they describe a deepening sense of consciousness, as the awareness of the unconscious enlarges the vision of oneself, of others and of the world.

This leaves Fowler's 'stage 6' (Universalizing Faith) on its own, but as a useful metaphor to accompany the final stages of maturity outlined in Erikson's view of integrity, Jung's concept of individuation, and Kohlberg's 'stage 7'. Here the universal is a common theme in all the models, to which I add a fourth life theme, that of letting go. In chapter 7 I examine these issues, suggesting that they represent ideals of which we catch active glimpses from time to time both in our own lives and in the lives of others. I shall suggest also that this last stage has sufficient links with the initial stages of life to provide a circularity which breaks away from the linear model, so that life at its end shares as much in its beginning, as the different stages of life share in each other.

1. D. Cupitt, *Life Lines* (SCM Press 1986), frontispiece.
2. D. Capps, *Life Cycle Theory and Pastoral Care* (Fortress Press 1983), p. 21.
3. M. Jacobs, *The Presenting Past* (Open University Press 1986), pp. 7–8.

4. Designed by Isabel Briggs Myers, Palo Alto, California (Consulting Psychologists Press 1977).
5. E. Erikson, *Childhood and Society* (Penguin 1965), p. 265 (footnote).
6. Joan Hemenway, 'Four Faith Frameworks' (*Journal of Pastoral Care*, XXXVIII, 4, 1984, pp. 317–23). Also in M. Jacobs (ed.), *Faith or Fear* (Darton Longman and Todd 1987), pp. 109–14.
7. Hemenway, op. cit., p. 322.
8. ibid., p. 317.
9. See also M. Jacobs, 'Naming and Labelling' (*Contact*, 3, 1976); *The Presenting Past*, pp. 22–4.
10. E. Belotti, *Little Girls* (London, Readers and Writers Co-operative, 1985). N. Chodorow, *The Reproduction of Mothering* (University of California Press 1978).
11. N. Golan, *Passing Through Transitions* (Collier Macmillan 1981).
12. Carol Gilligan, *In a Different Voice: Psychological Theory and Women's Development* (Harvard University Press 1982).
13. S. Freud, *New Introductory Lectures on Psychoanalysis* (Penguin 1973).
14. Gal. 3:28 (NEB).
15. J. W. Fowler, *Becoming Adult, Becoming Christian* (Harper and Row, San Francisco, 1984), p. 46.
16. Col. 3:11 (NEB).
17. J. W. Fowler, *Stages of Faith: the Psychology of Human Development and the Quest for Meaning* (San Francisco, Harper and Row, 1981), pp. 92–3.
18. L. Kohlberg, *The Philosophy of Moral Development* (San Francisco, Harper and Row, 1981), p. 323.
19. W. Cantwell Smith, *Faith and Belief* (Princeton University Press 1979), pp. 5–6.
20. For example, among others, Walter Hilton and Teresa of Avila.

4

Origins

Basic Images

Adult men and women do not like being thought of as having childish or even childlike qualities, but if we are to understand growth towards maturity, it is essential to start with themes that themselves begin in the initial moments of infancy. It is in those earliest months and years of human life that foundations are set for later life. What is 'learned' by experience as a helpless baby has a profound influence on the eventual adult that a child becomes. In particular, the images of mother and father formed in early experience continue to inform an adult's experience of self, of others, of the world, and of God. The sense of trust which is built (or not built) in primary relationships, influences values, attitudes and faith. The quality of these relationships promotes (or does not promote) both the discovery of the first stirrings of the self, and at the same time an early ability to empathize and identify with other people, which in its turn forms a basis for moral development that moves beyond self-interest and externalized imperatives to genuine concern.

It is important to make it clear that the early stages of development are never totally left behind, even though they are complemented by additional dimensions that come later. The main themes of the early stages of life continue to develop through childhood and adulthood. These themes, of trust, of care, of love, of dependence and dependability, all of which are linked to our first relationships, are significant (even if sometimes in their absence) for every person. In this chapter, therefore, I do not simply have in mind those whom, with Paul, we might call 'infants in Christ',[1] children and those adults who have no wish for more solid food. The themes apply as much to those who have a more complex understanding of faith. Pastoral care involves meeting all types of faith, and what I write here may throw light on both the simple and the complex. There are in fact similarities between this early stage and the final stages of maturity, not just in the sense that old age is sometimes called a second childhood. In faith terms the two ages share an ability to use images and symbols that is not restricted by the necessity to be rational, as well as a sense of one-ness with the world about them. There are, of course, significant differences, notably that maturity and mature faith are informed by preceding life experience, whereas infancy and simple faith are more limited in experience; but there is sufficient in common for the uncomplicated faith and values of those of simple faith to be as profound as the faith of those who have travelled a long way upon the spiritual journey. Indeed, the reader may detect a greater affection in me for these early stages than for the more conventional ones that I describe in the next chapter. This affection is not, I think, based upon a wish to return to the ignorance of bliss, because I am also aware of the need, in pastoral care, to assist those who wish it to move from one kind of profound, simple faith to another, equally profound, but more comprehensive expression of faith.

Although I subscribe to the view that images of God are projections of early experience, I do not imply that this type of faith is necessarily infantile. It is no more 'immature' than using metaphors in everyday speech to describe different experiences, because generally we prefer more graphic terms to abstract concepts. The latter may be intellectually correct, but they are less than complete in their power to evoke the fullness of experience. It is necessary, however, particularly when tracing the development of maturity, as well as in pastoral care, to distinguish between those who know when they are using images and metaphors and those who have no need to make such distinctions. The pastoral task is different with each type. In the case of those with profound, yet simple faith, pastoral care consists mainly of 'allowing persons to be where they are. If where they are meets their needs sufficiently, we can affirm them and their world-view out of our own experience that . . . symbols once met all our needs and . . . remain meaningful to us'.[2] Pastoral care of those who look for stronger meat also means engaging with people where they are, but this may well be a more turbulent, painful and yet ultimately more satisfying experience, especially if the pastor is at a similar stage of faith development. I do not believe that a pastor can be of real assistance to either type of person until he or she has had sufficient personal experience of the journey of faith to be able to recognize that there are differences.

In fact it is not just images of God and other religious beliefs that are founded in the early experience of the baby, since the relationship with 'mother' (still, in a more role-conscious age, the most convenient term for the nurturing person) also forms the basis for belief in self, and trust in the world in which we live, move and have our being. That this is so comes from the experience of a baby that the only world is the one which exists between her/himself and mother. It is the experience of the original microcosmic world of infancy, that is the whole world to a baby, that often colours attitudes to self, others and the world during the whole of adult life. As the child's world expands, the world that enlarges is the world that the baby originally perceived. Just as a picture on a rubber balloon grows in size as the balloon does, so the larger a child's world grows, the original perceptions of that world stay attached to it, growing larger, if fainter. These perceptions may make the expanding world even more enriching or even more terrifying, or probably a mixture of both. As the boundaries of that world begin to take in other people, as well as the church, religion, and God, all these are coloured in the same way. It is not surprising, then, that for some people God remains a projection of early childhood experience, with his (or perhaps her) form taken from those original images of mother and father.

Freud was certainly not the first to point to God being a figure made up of the projection of human fears and wishes, although it has been his particular critique of religion which seems to have made the most impact on twentieth-century thought. The nineteenth-century philosopher Feuerbach, earlier than Freud, was one of many who have suggested that God is nothing more than a projection of human imagination, but Freud followed this line of reasoning with a psychological explanation for the phenomenon. This was that the child in the adult needs to perpetuate an image of the omniscient and omnipotent parent, which the child is forced to give up when he or she recognizes that parents are fallible and imperfect. God can therefore be seen as a type of super-parent, who imparts some sense of order and protection and security in a hostile world. God goes on looking after us, long after our parents have ceased to do so.

Freud, in all his writings, emphasized the role of the father rather than the mother, and it is not surprising that he, like his religion of childhood, therefore saw God as a father-figure. It was Freud's followers who suggested more emphasis should be given to the study of the mother-baby relationship. Certainly by starting with the first stage of life, known in Freudian (and Erikson) terms as the oral stage, it is appropriate to look at the way in which the mother-baby relationship influences not only personal development but also the first stirrings of faith.

A study of hospital patients' views of God (I presume that they were mental hospital patients, although this is not clear in the report) has indicated that mothers figure just as greatly as fathers in perceptions of God. The study[3] showed a significant correlation for the hospital patients (and a non-significant correlation for a control church group) that God is identified in terms of people's actual earthly parents. They also found that the images of God were more influenced by earthly parents than by formal religious instruction. The authors of the study believe that by the time a child is introduced to the Church, the image of God is fixed and difficult to reshape.[4]

This strikes me as a pessimistic outlook, which condemns people to unchanging perpetuation of images of God that might be negative and harmful. While I accept the slowness with which most people change, I also want to make room for the development of maturity that can come about through new and different experiences of loving and accepting relationships later in life. This certainly happens in the context of good counselling and psychotherapy, and pastors will have their own examples of people whose negative perceptions and outlook have been changed through contact with or membership of a caring church. Indeed, in religious terms this is sometimes described as rebirth, a metaphor which is expressive and valuable as long as it is not confused with that zealous and narrow 'born-again' type of religion which often seems to forget that 'growing again' has to follow being born again, and that this is a long process!

At the same time, it is foolish to ignore the importance of early experience, in what may be a vain hope that later in life new relationships or the right type of pastoral care and counselling will help people to find more positive and trusting images of God. It may be that pastoral care needs to pay even more attention to the opportunities provided by contact with new parents and their children, in baptism or blessing of children, and in what might be offered to young families. Given the essential part which these early relationships play in laying the foundations for trust and love, this would appear to be a fruitful area of pastoral care, the significance of which has not yet been fully realized. It is not in Sunday Schools or Children's Church that children first learn about faith. The psychoanalyst Donald Winnicott, in a talk given to a conference on Family Evangelism[5] about the way children learn, said 'we are believing people because we were started off well by somebody. We received a silent communication over a long period of time that we were loved in the sense that we could rely on the environmental provision and so get on with *our own* growth and development' (my italics).

Winnicott stresses elsewhere in his writing that a 'facilitating environment' is essential to healthy development. In making this point he further assists the practice of pastoral care, confirming that 'being with' and providing a safe, 'holding' presence helps people to learn more about ultimate qualities such as faith, hope and love, than any amount of teaching and preaching. Only 'on the basis of what has been experienced by an individual', Winnicott said to the same conference, '[can we] teach the concept of, say, the everlasting arms'. He also seems to be saying that if we provide the right kind and degree of support, people will have sufficient security and the freedom to do their own growing and developing. Pastoral care does not consist of forcing people to develop as clone-like copies of what we ourselves imagine Christians should be.

Although he was brought up as a Methodist, Winnicott did not call himself a Christian. Speaking to a different audience at an earlier date, he was more critical of religion, and suggested an alternative to the communication of faith and moral sense by the teaching of religion, whether by brute force, or by more subtle means. 'The good alternative has to do with the provision of those conditions for the infant and child that enable such things as trust and "belief in", and ideas of right and wrong, to develop out of the working of the individual child's inner processes.'[6] Given a start in life which involves being cared for in a reliable way, 'the idea of goodness and of a reliable and personal parent or God can follow naturally'.[7]

This initial stage, in Fowler's faith development terms, is called stage 0. In refusing to give it a definite number Fowler perhaps wishes to represent that faith in the earliest stages of all cannot be properly defined, nor separated from the mother–baby relationship. The term he uses to describe stage 0 is 'undifferentiated faith'. The early months gives rise to what he calls the first pre-images of God, 'pre-' because as yet there is no language to describe real images. These pre-images emerge from the experience of the mutual relationship of mother and baby, in which a baby has her or his first awareness of a rudimentary sense of self separate from and yet dependent upon others.[8] Agreeing with Winnicott, Erikson and psychoanalytic opinion generally, Fowler sees this initial period as one where the seeds of trust, courage, love and hope are sown. Faber,[9] who draws heavily upon Erikson, also suggests that the relationship with mother is essential for the capacity to trust, to believe, and (he quotes Tillich's phrase) 'the courage to be'. He too stresses the need for trust to be built up if the child is to become emancipated from the mother, and to move from dependence to independence. He sums up the mother–child relationship at its best, using a German word that Freud also used, as one of 'bliss' or 'peace' – originally, as Faber says, a religious term.

Images in Religious Experience

It is scarcely surprising, then, that religious thought and feeling is sometimes expressed in language which speaks of a state of bliss, reminiscent of that symbiotic unity of love and knowing which at times exists between a mother and her baby. I have to say, especially as a man (because men are prone to sentimentalize motherhood!) that this is not a complete picture of the experience of mother and baby, although for the present I stay with it, because of its strong influence on religious thought and feeling. That there is another side to the experience of nurturing and being nurtured cannot be forgotten, and mature religious thinking certainly embraces the less idealized experiences of infancy.

We do not have to look far for evidence, amongst the symbols and images used to describe religious and mystical experience, which confirms the view of the developmental psychologists that early infancy is significant for the development of religious faith. There are strong elements in all religions (although in some more than in others, and particularly in the Catholic expression of Christianity) that are drawn from maternal and nurturing images and symbols. God is the provider and sustainer; feeding and comforting feature in descriptions of the divine. In primitive or naturalistic religion nurturing and sustaining is often expressed through nature gods, such as earth goddesses; and in animism there is a sense of intimate unity with the natural world, the womb of humankind. In different religious traditions, communion with the divine and with each other takes place through the act of feeding. This symbolism is particularly profound within the Christian tradition in the Eucharist. The traditional symbol for Corpus Christi is the female pelican suckling her young from the blood drawn from her own breast; the parallel to a human mother's breast is plain enough, and I do not think it takes anything away from what is probably one of the most powerful Christian phrases, 'This is my Body,' to link it with the way a mother offers her breast and her milk to her baby, in an act which is in some way experienced by a baby as equally sacrificial and sacred.

Even if God is sometimes portrayed in the Judaeo-Christian tradition as a distant and stern father-figure, or more positively as a forgiving father who runs to meet the prodigal son, other religions place greater emphasis upon the feminine in the Godhead or amongst the gods. Feminist theologians have sought to draw out the more latent images which show the feminine side of God, to counterbalance the masculine images which have dominated our own tradition,[10] although this way of seeing the Godhead as inclusive of both genders is not simply a modern phenomenon. Dame Julian of Norwich saw the motherhood of God at work in creation, and went so far as to call Jesus 'Mother of mercy'.[11] Meister Eckhart used a feminine form for 'Godhead'. More commonly within the Christian tradition, the figure of Mary has been the closest approximation to a mother God – hence the discomfort of some Protestants about the feelings which Catholics express towards her. The idealization of the state of motherhood finds its full flower in the all-too-often generally sanitized pictures of a gentle Mary, where the reality of mothering, with its pain and frustrations as well as its joys, is almost totally ignored. The image of the mother of Jesus at the foot of the cross, or holding the body of her dead son, is the nearest we get to an expression of the other side – of the pain of motherhood.

It is this exaggerated imagery of Virgin-mother and Child which might lead one to dismiss the maternal images in religious thought and feeling as pure phantasy. In Freud's more negative view, the oceanic feeling which is experienced in religious ecstasy is reduced to a wish to return to highest moments of unity between mother and baby. The same experience is seen much more positively by Erikson, who writes of 'the simple and fervent wish for a hallucinatory sense of unity with the maternal matrix.'[12] In the same passage, he sees no reason why we should call it regression if 'man thus seeks again the earliest encounters of his trustful past in his efforts to reach for a hoped-for and eternal future'. At its best, religion helps us to go back to early experiences, and to work with some of the issues that concerned us then and still concern us now.

In public worship and in private devotion these images and symbols are especially important, even if there is always a danger that images can become idols, and symbols become substitutes, which Erikson would call the 'excess ritual' of the numinous stage. In the planning and conduct of worship, and in the decoration of churches or places that are used for private prayer and times of quiet, there are endless opportunities for tasteful and intelligent use of imagery and symbolism as a focus not only for people's attention, but also for their projections. Music is particularly evocative, perhaps because its medium of communication is non-verbal, and closer to the use of tone and sound (more than specific words) in the interaction between mother and baby.

Worship feeds people in all sorts of ways, but it especially helps meet our wishes for dependency and dependability, as well as for a sense of oneness with the transcendent and with each other, and for feelings of being accepted and being loved. This is not unhealthy or immature in itself. The spirit needs as much feeding as the body. Worship, like the arts or the natural world, can evoke feelings as well as thoughts which take us close to transcendent experience. Even hard-nosed agnostics can say, 'That was a lovely service.' Public worship provides the pastoral ministry with opportunities and rich sources, sometimes of comfort, sometimes of challenge, and always of potential ways of understanding ourselves and our world. It is important that symbols and images, and prayer and worship, do not remain ends in themselves. They should not encourage denial of the reality of life and of the world we live in. At the same time symbols can expand the horizons of reality and lead us into our own dark corners of denial. The fascination of images and pictures in the early stages of personal and faith development is a first step towards a more mature use of images in later stages.

I believe it is important in worship to be capable (at least at times) of suspending reason, and so not to be too troubled by words, phrases and actions which, in other contexts, are open to question and clarification. At the same time the experience of some aspects of worship may produce new ways of 'seeing', which can be expressed later in more rational language. It is difficult to describe, and certainly impossible to prescribe, the right balance between thinking and feeling, and the degree of suspension of rationality that is necessary in worship, but perhaps a parallel can be drawn from the experience of live theatre. There too members of the audience have to some extent to suspend reason, to believe in what takes place on the stage, and yet also to know that it is not true, so that they are taken beyond the drama into a deeper experience and understanding of themselves and others. My own conviction is that if we are going to restore the value of religious thought and feeling to many of those who now rightly question the literalism of our Christian tradition, we have to make clear, even from time to time in conducting worship, that our images point beyond themselves to truths which people will interpret, as appropriate, in their own way. Worship is a corporate activity in which those present need to discover their own individual insights into the collective phantasies to which expression is given.

Avoiding Reality

I mentioned above that there is another side to the experience of infancy and of mothering, far removed from the idealized pictures people have of that time of life and of that first relationship. This other side has to be taken fully into account if we are to understand balanced development towards maturity. It is a corrective to too much attention to images of bliss.

Like Erikson I would not want to label as neurotic or regressive the type of religious imagery that apparently expresses the wish to return to the blissful times in infancy. The Garden of Eden has been so strongly guarded by the cherubim and the flaming sword[13] that it is actually impossible to go back to such states of happiness for long. Fowler reminds us of the other side to the experience of infancy, when he expands his picture of undifferentiated faith to include a baby having to contend with the threat (in fact or phantasy) of abandonment, inconsistency and deprivation. He uses a theological term to describe this experience, calling it a fall from grace, a type of primal Fall into consciousness, as the baby realizes that he is not at the centre of the world, that he needs others, and that others are separate beings. Psychoanalytic thought certainly concurs that the dawning of this realization occurs when a baby begins to perceive that mother is a separate person, and not always 'on tap'. Bliss often has to alternate with experiences of deprivation or hell, vividly portrayed in the contrast between the thirst of Dives, and Lazarus 'in Abraham's bosom'.[14] The breast, which the baby so much needs and desires for psychological as well as physical reasons, sometimes provides succour and a sense of well-being. At other times, however, the same breast is withheld, giving rise to a totally different set of experiences in the child, which are reflected in adult experiences of emptiness and lack of self-worth.

The sublimity of stage 0 undifferentiated faith soon gives way to these other aspects, which start a child on the road towards facing both the reality of the separateness of the world and of others, and the frustration that is as much part of life as is satisfaction. Trust, according to Faber,[15] includes more than ultimate security and the capacity to receive love; it also involves delight in reality, the integration of negative experiences, and the capacity not to be overwhelmed by fear or aggression. It is this other side of the picture which deserves our attention, because personal maturity involves being able to integrate the light and the shadow (in Jungian terms), or good and bad experiences (in more psychoanalytic terms). This lifelong task, begun in infancy, can be hindered or helped by religious faith.

The inability to face frustrations, the fear of angst and aggression, of sexuality and tenderness, and the impossibility of reconciling good and bad experiences often lead to different types of personal difficulty, and to what I believe are travesties of faith. My concern is with healthy development more than with pathological features, and I do not wish to dwell on the distortions. Nevertheless it might be helpful to illustrate briefly what I mean. Faber reminds us that failure of trust can lead to other experiences of mother (as bad) and to a different set of phantasies, which still have an oral (feeding) character, particularly the fear of being devoured. This fear is reflected in fairy tales where children are abandoned by their parents (often by mother), and are at risk of being devoured by some evil figure like a witch, giant, or wolf. The same anxious imagery is there in religious phrases such as 'the jaws of death', or the 'jaws of the grave'. The Compline sentence too, speaks of being wary of the devil, who like a lion, prowls around, seeking whom he may *devour*. At the same time, Faber observes that death can be seen in much more comforting terms in oral imagery, with the tomb equated with the womb.[16]

Failure to trust (based perhaps on experiences in childhood) may lead to distorted pictures of God. Although it is not an example from this early stage of development, Justice and Lambert illustrate how incest victims can have a distorted view of God and of God's love – showing how dangerous it might be with some people to use human images of God. 'When I hear you say that God loves me, I have a hard time trying not to remember Daddy raping me and saying, "I love you, I love you, I love you all" – all the time he was doing it to me . . . Even after all these years, every time I hear the word God, I see Daddy's face.'[17]

This bleak picture is a less comforting example of the influence of childhood experiences on the formation of images of God. With such negative experiences of trust, we can see how unbelief, and not just belief, can result from experience of bad parenting. Faber mentions a book on *The Psychology of Unbelief*[18] in which Rumke argues that it is unbelief, and not belief, which indicates a disturbance in development.

There are numerous responses to the 'fall from grace' that is an integral part of the earliest weeks of infancy (and which, of course, is no one's *fault*, but an inevitable part of growing consciousness). Fowler suggests two negative directions in which faith can develop from the pre-faith stage 0. One consists of the feelings of isolation and mistrust already alluded to above. The other is excessive narcissism, where the need to be at the centre of everything continues to dominate, and where the phantasy persists that God is at one's beck and call. In its most extreme form it is seen in those who claim divinity for themselves – often, of course, people with psychotic or borderline personalities. There is also a narcissistic element in the way some people expect the Church to be an extension of themselves, and need other people to believe what they believe; or in those who show a degree of enthusiasm and fanaticism which boosts their own ego more it than promotes the kingdom of God. For such people resistance of their demands, or the failure of God to answer their prayers, can lead to a damaging wound to their self-esteem, based as it is on narcissistic selfishness more than on genuine self-love. The fanatical zeal to convert others, and make them the same as themselves is different in quality from the more conformist type of religion, typified in the 'anal stage' themes of authority and autonomy.

There is a further unsatisfactory way of coping with the 'fall from grace', which needs to be added to these two negative directions. Psychologically it is known as splitting, a term which describes the attempt to cope with the difficulty of understanding how good and bad experiences can come from the same source (e.g. mother or the breast). One way of understanding such a contradiction, is to imagine that there must be one bad mother responsible for all the frustration and pain, and another mother, a good one, who is responsible for all the warmth and love. In healthy development this splitting is gradually set aside as no longer a viable explanation, as a child realizes that parents (and by implication therefore the world, others and the self) are both good and bad. Despair is felt if the bad seems stronger than the good, hope if the good is felt to outweigh the bad.

Here we have, in psychological form, the most taxing of all theological questions. How can a good God (like a good mother) allow such bad things to happen? Splitting is seen in faith terms in belief in good and evil powers, and in the struggle between God and the Devil, in the existence of demi-gods, and in other examples of dualistic religion, which, at times, have been evident in Christian tradition. I do not suggest that a problem which has vexed the mightiest theological minds is capable of easy solution, but in psychological terms, a healthy solution has to include the recognition that there can only be one God, to whom must be ascribed both positive and negative, good and bad.

This is simply, but profoundly, expressed when a person – as it may seem to a more 'reasonable' observer – almost simplistically believes that all things, however bad they seem, come from a good God. Baldridge and Gleason[19] give an example of Tillich's World-view A person, a grandmother who has lost nearly all her family in a succession of deaths. Yet she can still say with complete conviction that what has happened is all God's will, and that the Lord is good to her. What makes her simple faith so mature is that she does *not* see the deaths of her relatives as a punishment. If she did, that would be another form of splitting: God is good and I am bad, so I deserve this treatment. She provides a superb example of the way in which a literal, undeveloped and unquestioning faith (which is actually very rare), can sometimes express just as mature a psychological truth as a more complex set of beliefs. The old woman's simple faith gave her the ability to reconcile bad experiences with a good God, and at the same time retain a good self-image.

Needless to say, this task of unifying experience, and of integrating good and bad, is not one which is resolved in infancy, although it is in infancy and childhood that the process is begun. These issues continue to present themselves at all later stages, and particularly in the second half of life. Adolescents learn that elation and despair are both part of life's experience; couples in love learn to integrate the reality of each other's faults with their initial idealization of each other; parents learn that children can be both very good, and also very horrid; and older people recognize that their lives, as they reflect upon them, are full of good and bad moments, successes and failures. In healthy development and relationships, the balance comes down in favour of the positive, but without the more negative aspects being split off or ignored.

Religion – Illusion and Reality

Despite the painfulness of her situation, there is a beauty in the example of grandmother's simple belief that all her family disasters were part of God's good will. She does not ascribe human motives to God, nor attempt a more rational explanation of her fate. She is unusual, because many people could not answer the question 'Why?' in her way without being led on to other more complex questions about the purposes and the goodness of God.

Her literal belief (in Tillich's terms), and her contentment with a 'simple' answer to the question of her suffering both show resemblances to some of the features in Fowler's next stage of the faith development model, the first definite stage called 'intuitive-projective faith'. While this stage is not chronologically coterminous with Erikson's first age, there are many features of Fowler's description which show psychological similarities with 'oral stage' themes of trust and dependency and of the first discovery of a sense of self. Fowler describes children as asking questions but at the same time finding difficulty both in understanding the relation between cause and effect, and in maintaining more than one perspective on experience at a time. This struggling to make sense of experience, is also present before questions can be framed in words, but with the advent of language explanations can be more easily sought and more easily given. In developmental terms, children ask deep questions, but are often satisfied with a simple, intelligible answer. In faith terms too, there are some people, whose deep questions are readily answered, without the obsessive need for textual proof or quasi-historical truth which is much more typical of the Tillich World-view B person, struggling to hold on to literalism and afraid to move into the stage of doubt that in itself brings new insights.

Stage 1 is a time filled with phantasy, where a child is powerfully and permanently influenced by examples, moods, actions and stories coming from adults. With unrestrained imagination, uninhibited by logical thought as adults understand it (although the child's thought can often be seen to have a logic of its own), a child at this stage grasps the world of experience intuitively. Fairy stories, and certain Bible stories, may help the child to believe that good can win over bad. The danger of this stage is that a child's imagination becomes possessed by unrestrained and uncorrected images of terror and destructiveness. Adults may exploit a child's imagination, reinforcing taboos and moral and doctrinal expectations with images of punishment, the devil and death.

If images and symbols matter as greatly as they do, then it is clearly important to make positive use of story telling in pastoral teaching and preaching. If stories feed the imagination of the child, and the adult, providing the raw material for the development of their own phantasies, the use of story in preaching and teaching needs to be treated with care, so that stories impart confidence rather than fear. In so doing, pastoral care can help people move beyond the 'fear' motivation for moral decisions and action which is also typical of the first stage of the Kohlberg scheme.

In pastoral care we meet some people who take their images and symbols literally. It is important to bear in mind that they may reach a time when they begin to 'see through' the symbols. How can pastoral care prepare them for that time, without pushing them into it? On discovering that something is not true, a person can feel so disappointed, deceived and let down, that the value of the symbol is lost, perhaps for ever, and confidence in the purveyor of the symbol (e.g. the Church) is broken. This happens (though less today perhaps than a few years ago) with children who really believe in Father Christmas, and who feel a sense of loss of faith in adults when the secret comes out. Yet they tend not to experience such a loss of confidence in relation to fairy stories that have always been told to them *as if* they were true, but with an underlying assumption that they are not true.

Stories need to be told, as fairy stories themselves are, for their underlying truth more than for their factual reality. That way adults will be able to go on loving and using the religious stories they have learned as children, without having to strain their credulity or their confidence in the integrity of belief. As adults we have little difficulty drawing upon fairy stories and folk myths, seeing them as outside time and reality, not rooted in historical events yet no less valuable for all that. The concern for historical accuracy in the Church has so often robbed the Judaeo-Christian stories of their timeless richness.

'Seeing through' images can mean looking beyond them, rather than being disappointed at the dawning realization that a symbol is nothing in itself. Perhaps there would be less sense, in both growing children and adults, of having been 'taken for a ride' by the literal use of symbolic language and images, if in both worship and pastoral conversation more care were taken to convey the 'not quite true' (or what psychoanalysis would call the 'as if') quality of religious language and symbols. Pastors need to be concerned for those who actually have serious doubts about some of the language used in prayers and hymns and credal definitions, and who are often prevented from 'seeing through' these images, symbols and metaphors to deeper meanings, because they have not been told that it is unnecessary to take them literally.

So a child's world is full of symbols, some of which are religious, some of which are from fairy tales, some of which are from other aspects of the prevailing culture. In the very early months symbols are pre-verbal, but as the child grows and hears stories, and develops stories in her/his own imagination, he or she is involved in an attempt to make sense of conflicting and sometimes anxiety-provoking experiences, using phantasy and powerful images to do so. In many respects it is a delightful stage, when everything and anything can be believed, no matter how contradictory the different statements may appear to the adult. It is the images that capture the imagination, and not the specifically religious messages that go with them. It is a stage which William James, affectionately quoted by Fowler, called 'blooming, buzzing confusion'!

Symbols remain powerful throughout life for most of us, whatever our personal belief system may be. However, it is rare that adults, or even older children, stay in this particular stage of faith, because symbols gradually need to be ordered, and made to hang together, as they do in myths and stories. Even the most simple faith of adults is more like Fowler's stage 2 faith (to be explained in the next chapter) than stage 1. But even in stage 2, images and symbols are taken literally, with evidence of the richness of imagination sometimes seen in fantastic 'pictures' of God, seen not only in children's descriptions of God when still at the Piagetian stage of intuitive thinking, but also in the more traditional mythologies of world religions, including the Judaeo–Christian tradition.

Phantasy plays a very important part in psychological development, so we might expect it also to be significant in faith development. The child analyst Donald Winnicott values phantasy highly, and describes the initial task of a mother as one of creating a sense of illusion for her baby, the illusion that the baby has control of the breast.[20] Illusion is used by Winnicott in a much more positive sense than in Freud's assumption that illusion, including religion, is an escape from reality. Winnicott recognizes that the reality of the mother's inevitable absence when she is needed is too painful for a helpless baby to bear. The illusion that she is part of the baby has to be created, if she is later to disillusion her baby so as to be able to tolerate reality. In order to disillusion the baby gradually, the mother introduces what Winnicott has called 'a transitional object' – a dummy, a cuddly toy, or a piece of muslin or blanket. The transitional object represents a type of intermediate reality. Only later, if the transitional object itself is not given up, does it become like a fetish, and foster delusion.

The last paragraph will appear very technical and a long way from pastoral care, but the pastor has the same task of helping people to face reality. Christianity is not an escape from the harshness of the world. Religious imagery has a positive illusory quality to it, that helps people to accommodate themselves to the harshness of reality, and to the anxieties arising from the emptiness and loss of meaning that sometimes accompany the awareness of reality. In their own way reality, and the anxiety that accompanies the uncovering of it, can be as terrifying in adult life as they are in infancy. A universal example of this is the growing awareness of the reality of being finite and mortal, which often niggles at the self-centredness that is typical of the first half of life but does not truly begin to dawn in most people before middle age. Religion can be a valuable illusion, and its symbols and beliefs can provide transitional objects, because, as Winnicott writes, 'no human being is free from the strain of relating inner and outer reality . . . relief from this strain is provided by an intermediate area of experience which is not challenged (arts, religion, etc.)'.[21] In better known words, T. S. Eliot expresses a similar view: 'humankind cannot bear very much reality'.[22]

Faber also draws upon Winnicott's writing on the success or failure of the transitional object, and notes the consequent success or failure of religion to help people face reality. He gives examples of transitional objects in religious use, particularly in Catholicism,[23] although he does not speak of images of God or of religion itself as transitional objects. I would myself argue that all the images of God which religion employs are transitional, representing intermediate reality, but never to be mistaken for reality itself. There are few things of which we can ever be certain, apart from death itself, but we can also be sure that no human being is ever knowledgeable enough to comprehend either the reality of life and death, or any reality that may lie beyond. Unfortunately too many people, in churches and outside them, speak as if they knew and understood reality, mistaking the transitional for reality itself.

Cupitt, though clearly conversant with psychoanalysis, does not indicate any knowledge of Winnicott even though he echoes the latter's sentiments. Cupitt suggests that, since mother 'is not around all or much of the time, [the baby] must eventually frame some kind of world-hypothesis which postulates her identity and continuity between her appearances. This may be connected with faith in the power of the Word, i.e. how reliably she appears when he yells.'[24] This interweaving of illusion and reality, whether in Winnicott and Cupitt, or indeed in the use of human and earthly images to tolerate the inability to understand and know the transcendent, is more than a psychological truth. It can be supported from a theological viewpoint too, because although theologians may differ in their explanations and descriptions of God, they are united in agreeing that all language applied to God is metaphorical. When God is described as Mother or Father or by some less personal image, or when the qualities of God are described in language reminiscent of relations between people or between things, such descriptions have to be seen as having a transitional quality. It is easy to forget in pastoral ministry, where God-talk is so much part of the stock-in-trade, that all language about God is weak and is bound at some point to fail; and to forget that many people who are less used to God-talk, like the little boy who declares the Emperor has no clothes, see its flaws more obviously.

Winnicott, upon whose work on infancy I have drawn in this chapter, once commented upon his Wesleyan Methodist origins, 'I am always glad that my religious upbringing was of a kind that allowed for growing up out of.'[25] This stage of development, growing up out of conventional religion, is one to which I turn in subsequent chapters, but it is a future possibility which continuously needs to be kept in mind even when thinking about the themes of trust and dependency, and about the building of the basis of faith. I have made it obvious that I believe pastoral care can make rich use of phantasy and illusion without selling itself short. The human images and symbols of love, trust, dependency and dependability, of feeding, nurturing, and of care, interweave with religious hope and faith, and therefore need to be communicated, as far as is humanly possible, in word and attitude, in formal worship and in casual encounter.

At the same time the rich imagery and symbols of the religious and the personal, the human and the divine need to be conveyed in such a way, that there is always the possibility of learning to see them as transitional, particularly when people later reach a more deeply questioning stage of development. If the images and metaphors are always put across as if they are literally true, and as if they are unquestionable, or if they are conveyed as ends in themselves, we may even prevent some people from developing a more mature faith, because they do not think they are allowed to give up the images of childhood. They are so tied to them that they never 'grow up out of' phantasy to ask the questions evoked by the realities of life in the world.

Others whom we meet in pastoral care impulsively reject the faith which is being offered them as childish and untenable, and are not helped to look beyond their present worldly realities (which they do face) to more ultimate reality, of which so much religion makes them only dimly aware. There is an urgent pastoral task that needs to be addressed, of providing the right environment in which some people (though not necessarily all) will find encouragement to 'grow up out of' the literalism of religious language, and to use these transitional stepping stones of basic human images towards the discovery and integration of deeper, more complex questions about life and faith.

1. 1 Cor. 3:2. See also 1 Pet. 2:2.
2. W. E. Baldridge and J. J. Gleason, 'A Theological Framework for Pastoral Care' (*The Journal of Pastoral Care*, XXXII, 4, 1978, p. 237).
3. W. G. Justice, and W. Lambert, 'A Comparative Study of the

Language People use to Describe the Personalities of God and their Earthly Parents' (*The Journal of Pastoral Care*, xxxx, 2, 1986, pp. 166–172).

4. See also Anna-Maria Rizzuto, *The Birth of the Living God* (University of Chicago Press 1979).
5. D. W. Winnicott, *Home is Where We Start From* (Penguin 1986), pp. 141–50.
6. D. W. Winnicott, *The Maturational Processes and the Facilitating Environment* (Tavistock Publications 1965), p. 94.
7. ibid., p. 97.
8. J. W. Fowler, *Stages of Faith: the Psychology of Human Development and the Quest for Meaning* (San Francisco, Harper and Row, 1981), p. 121.
9. H. Faber, *Psychology of Religion* (SCM Press 1976).
10. See a particularly useful summary of arguments for, and images of, the motherhood of God in chapter 4, 'God as Mother' in S. McFague, *Models of God* (Fortress Press and SCM Press 1987). See also K. Leech, *True God* (Sheldon Press 1985), ch. 12, 'God the Mother'; and A. Loades, *Searching for Lost Coins* (SPCK 1987), ch. 5, 'God and god-ess'.
11. E. Colledge and J. Walsh (trans.), *Julian of Norwich: Showings* (Paulist Press and SPCK 1978), ch. 59. For a summary see J. Gatta, *A Pastoral Art* (Darton Longman and Todd 1987), pp. 71–4.
12. E. Erikson, *Young Man Luther* (Faber 1959), p. 257.
13. Gen. 3:24 (AV).
14. Luke 16:20–24 (AV).
15. Faber, op. cit., p. 160.
16. ibid., p. 168.
17. Justice and Lambert, op. cit., p. 166.
18. Faber, op. cit., pp. 148–9.
19. Baldridge and Gleason, op. cit., p. 232.
20. D. W. Winnicott, 'Transitional Objects and Transitional Phenomena', *Collected Papers* (Tavistock Publications 1958), pp. 229–42.
21. ibid., p. 240.
22. T. S. Eliot, 'Burnt Norton' in *Four Quartets* (Faber 1959), p. 14.
23. Faber, op. cit., p. 166.
24. D. Cupitt, *Life-lines* (SCM Press 1986), p. 18.
25. Winnicott, *Home Is Where We Start From*, p. 142.

5

Conventions

Coming Together

The inclusion of transitional periods in Levinson's scheme of development and also the coining of the term 'transitional object' by Winnicott are both reminders of the gradualness of development, and of the absence of any clear division between the end of one stage and the start of another. In considering the next set of themes, which are principally to do with autonomy and authority, there is an obvious overlap with the position reached in the last chapter, as well as a pointer to the next, when reliance on external authority gives way to the development of an inner authority. In planning these chapters I toyed with placing Fowler's stage 2 in the first set of themes, because his title for this period of religious development, 'Mythic-Literal'[1] certainly embraces some of the features described amongst those themes. Out of the 'blooming, buzzing confusion' of the variety of symbols and images in Fowler's stages 0 and 1,[2] there is in stage 2 a bringing together of symbols into more continuous stories and myths.

But it is this bringing together which weighed in favour of my inclusion of stage 2 in this set of themes, because there is a sense of ordering which runs through 'anal stage' issues. This bringing together also explains my choice of 'Conventions' as the title of this chapter. It is a word which has two quite different meanings, both of which apply to autonomy and authority: firstly 'coming together', which I describe in this section; and secondly the idea of conforming to conventions, which forms the second major aspect of my description of this period of development.

The start of the second phase of personality development

(as in the Erikson model) also consists of a significant degree of coming together, in which some order is brought to bear upon both the functions and functioning of the body and upon making sense of experience. Controlling oneself, and to some extent controlling one's environment, are major issues, although autonomy also gives rise to problems of how far other people's control (like parental authority) has to be accepted, and how much it can be questioned.

The continuity which links these themes of autonomy and authority to the more narrow, and natural, concern for self in the first set of themes, and to the wider vision and concern of the later themes, is usefully described by Anna Freud[3] through the idea of developmental lines. These separate, though linked, lines illustrate how normal children move from basic elemental needs through to independence and socialization, from the original focus on the body and its functions, through to a wider interest and involvement in life as a whole. So, for instance, a developmental line can be traced from the most basic need to be fed, and the overwhelming significance of the actual or substitute breast, through weaning, to the ability to feed onself, to the use of 'tools' for eating, through struggles of will over eating, and gradually out of the intense (sexualized) pleasure that comes from food to what Guntrip describes, in one of several alternative definitions of a mature and stable person, as 'simple pleasure in eating and drinking according to his actual needs and pleasant company'.[4]

Although Anna Freud's line breaks off at that point, because her concern is with childhood, it is possible to extend it through adolescence, as the young person takes more responsibility for his or her diet, and for preparation and planning of meals, first for self and then for others, to the possibility of concern about whether other people, outside the family, have enough to eat, rather than preoccupation with one's own stomach.

A second developmental line includes the gradual acquisition of bladder and bowel control, which extends to taking over parental attitudes to cleanliness. Again I think it is possible to extend this line beyond childhood into adult life, with this line coming to fruition in concern for the cleanliness of the natural environment, about the 'waste' of resources, and over the way some waste products are partially destroying the world. (I return to this aspect below when describing Faber's equation of secularization with anal religion.) Here again the developmental line moves from self-interest, through to self-control and self-ordering, and then to concern for others, with my own extension taking the theme forwards to concern for society and the external world. The emphasis Anna Freud places on bowel and bladder is typical of her father's description of this particular stage of development. Erikson,[5] however, enlarges the scope of the anal stage to include muscular development generally, recognizing that this stage includes the achievement of many different kinds of control – such as the co-ordination of limbs, and the use of them to achieve greater independence, the ability to play with objects, to examine and explore them, and the use of such objects for games.

Anna Freud does not neglect this aspect, but makes it a separate developmental line, with the initial object of play being the body (for instance, fist or thumb), followed by the transitional object, then cuddly toys, which gradually give place to the inclusion of other toys. Through playing with toys a child achieves his or her first learning, seeing how objects move, how they can be taken apart, how they can be built up into larger objects. Toys also serve as a means of exploring sexuality and gender, as feminists have pointed out in criticizing the stereotyping of girls and boys by expecting them to play respectively with either dolls or soldiers. The line does not stop there, because the capacity to play is used in education and, in that context, is used to lead children into playing with words, numbers and eventually with ideas. In turn this learning, whether it is of the three Rs or of manual and technical skills, comes together with the ability to sustain work (with its frustrations as well as its satisfactions) in using skills to earn a living. These skills can also be used for the management and upkeep of home and garden, and for hobbies, pastimes and other interests.

The last of the developmental lines suggested by Anna Freud is one which moves from the egocentricity of infancy to the companionship and partnership of later childhood and into adult life. At first a child's natural preoccupation is with the self. Other children are then encountered, but as objects rather than as other individuals, to be pushed, picked up and dropped as much as toys might be. Then other children become companions in play, valuable more as assisting in carrying out tasks and playing games, rather than as later becoming friends in their own right. Again this line could be extended beyond childhood into adolescence, with its peer groups and development of closer relationships, to the stages of intimacy, where others may at first be sexual playthings, or partners in setting up home and family, before they are fully valued in their own right. If this developmental line is even further extended, to socialization generally in adult life, it surely comes to fruition in concern for others outside family, friends and work, for those who in one sense are faceless, because they are not personally known, but nevertheless can be felt for as fellow members of the same human race.

Such a whirlwind tour of the different lines of human development may have left the reader breathless, but it demonstrates the way in which the chaotic and uncontrollable world of the small baby gradually takes shape, begins to show evidence of control and order, and turns outward so that the growing skills and concerns can be more or less fully expressed in adult life. My own additions to the developmental lines indicate that it is possible to see them extending into wider concern than just for oneself or one's immediate family. Freud expressed the same possibility of the extension of childhood concerns into adult life through sublimation, for the promotion and service of society and culture, the arts, intellectual exploration, and technical and scientific achievement. That he did not extend sublimation to religion is perhaps due to his own acknowledged difficulties with that particular area of thinking.

As the body develops, and the muscles begin to respond to the wishes of the child, there is a growing sense of control and co-ordination. This is just as true of the inner world, because with the development of thinking and of language, there comes both the wish and the ability to begin to make some sense of experience, of rules of behaviour, and of the world all around. The chaotic world of the tiny infant, with its crude phantasies which serve, at least temporarily, to make sense of bewildering experiences, gives way to the ability and the wish to get things straight, to order and to understand, and to 'get things taped'.

This desire is so strong that some of what 'gets taped' sometimes takes a form which makes little sense to the adult, even though it gives a sense of order and cohesion to the child. There are phrases in the Lord's Prayer which provide a good example of the way children often turn what they have learnt into a form which they can understand, because the phrases as used by adults make no sense to them: 'Lead us not into Thames station', 'Vikings will come', and 'Harold be thy name', are examples I have myself come across. Children are often compelled – because not understanding makes them feel either anxious, or shameful, or both – to make some sense out of what they hear, by ordering it into a framework which they do understand.

The same applies to some adult 'rules' and codes of behaviour, which sometimes can be applied by a child in ways an adult thinks show misunderstanding, but which to a child are 'logically' consistent with all he or she has been told. Because children have only a limited number of ways of looking at issues, they often find it difficult to discriminate between the nuances of adult rules and behaviour. The expression, 'Don't do as I do, do as I say,' may well be how a child experiences the difference between a parent's injunctions and example. The rules adults impart to their children are inevitably simplifications of complex adult ways of behaving. 'But you told me I had to . . .'; 'Well I didn't mean that!' Needless to say, such misunderstandings can occur between adults too, and apparently mature men and women can find it difficult to see the nuances involved in moral thinking.

From the age of about two a child is involved in a huge task of learning. As they grow, children soak up knowledge, often know more facts about certain favourite topics than most adults do, and can play sophisticated games which require mental and physical co-ordination – again sometimes better than some adults. Little wonder then that a child works hard at sorting out what is real from what is make-believe. Images and symbols begin to be used to give some sense of meaning; but it is still the story that matters. There is as yet no stepping back from the story to reflect upon it, or to communicate the same meaning in abstract terms. Meaning can only be experienced in concrete terms. As Fowler puts it, 'meaning is both carried and "trapped" in the narrative'.[6]

So in Fowler's stage 2, the symbols and images which dominated the earlier Intuitive–Projective stage, begin to take more definite shape, as stories are assembled from them, and the images themselves are refined. As examples of this, Fowler shows how descriptions of God change as children move from stage 1 to stage 2, from what he calls nascent to more developed anthropomorphic images. Stage 1 thinking is represented by the answer Freddy gave to the question, 'What is God like?': 'He has a light shirt on, brown hair and brown eyelashes.'[7] There is nothing special about these images. Even if they show that Freddy is imaginative, he probably says the first thing that comes into his head, which is typical of the Intuitive-Projective stage. When Millie was asked the same question, she gave an answer which was indicative of stage 2 (the Mythic-Literal stage), describing God in much more conventional terms, perhaps influenced by the traditional pictures conveyed to her by parents, by the churches, and other adults, and in her case by television. But there is clear evidence that she was thinking more deeply about what she was saying, because she prefaced her description by saying she did not know the answer, and *knew* she was imagining:

> I don't know. But . . . I imagine that he's an old man with a white beard and white hair wearing a long robe, and that the clouds are his floor and he has a throne, and he has all these people and there's angels around him . . . he has a nice face and blue eyes . . . and he's forgiving.[8]

In this more developed set of images, God is still described as a man, but Millie's other answers revealed that God had more than physical atttributes. God is ascribed some personal qualities, like being forgiving. He can make mistakes like her parents do. Yet despite an apparently simple faith, there are signs in stage 2 of growing puzzlement. Concrete thinking has its weaknesses, and does not answer some questions. In stage 1 Freddy could answer the problem of how God, whom he saw as a man, can be everywhere, by saying without any sense of contradiction that God 'he can split up or he can be like God'.[9] In an example in Goldman's research, nine-year-old (equivalent stage 2) Peter cannot reconcile God being in one place, the Burning Bush, and everywhere at the same time.[10]

This stage of faith, accompanied by a straightforward trust in simple rules and in the fairness that comes from adhering to them, is found in some adolescents and adults as well as in children. I have already observed that Tillich's World-view A, the stage of natural or pre-conscious literalism, has distinct similarities to Fowler's stage 1, and the term 'literalism' also links to Fowler's 'Mythic-Literal' stage of faith. Cupitt,[11] describing the development of theology, writes of a stage of 'mythical realism', which again ties in with the stage of development being described at this point. He agrees that mythical realism is pictorial, and says that it is unsystematic, but only by later standards. 'Concern for the systematic organization of the self, of society, of the world, of life and time and of the religious realm itself is by no means absent. But it is still relatively weak, because the need for it has not yet been deeply felt.'[12] Baldridge and Gleason quote Tillich's similar words, that this stage, like the first, is 'still justifiable if the questioning power is very weak and can easily be answered'.[13]

Pastoral care of people at this stage is mainly that of older children and young adolescents, although some adults show signs of 'Mythic–Literal' faith. The encouragement of the growth towards maturity consists largely of using 'the emergence of story, drama and myth as ways of finding and giving coherence to experience'.[14] To help the coming together (the convention) of both children and adults so that they move from self-concern into a wider community of faith is obviously important, and to that end the stories of the Church will help create a sense of belonging and coherence. The problem for pastoral care is how to do this without appearing to provide such a coherent a picture of 'the faith', that will then be taken as a self-contained, closed system, which can provide the ready answers to any question or for any eventuality. The tradition of the Bible and the Church needs to be conveyed as a rich and valued, but varied resource, rich and valuable because of, and not in spite of, its contradictions. The difficulty for pastoral care at this point of personal development is how to help people 'converse' (come together, both in themselves, and with others) without becoming 'conventional'.

Conformity

Growing *up* also involves growing *into* a family, a community, and a society. The natural self-centredness of infancy, living as yet in a tiny 'world' that is easily confused with the self, has to give way to the wider world that also consists of the expectations, wishes and conventions of other people. We have to learn to accommodate ourselves to others, a process which brings pleasure to ourselves and others when we show the ability to do so, and which brings varying degrees of disapproval when we do not, or cannot. Life in a family, a community, and society therefore involves learning not just the folk-lore (the stories and images which the preceding section includes), but also folk-law, the rules and codes of behaviour which govern family and community life – many of which are not statutory or biblical rules, but are individual family and community interpretations of right and wrong. Learning to live with others starts with simple though effective understanding that various rewards and punishments accompany conformity to or rejection of their expectations. Children often find it difficult to understand reasons, but they do understand pleasure and displeasure. Fear and bargaining (Kohlberg's first two stages of moral development) give way to conformity, and the wish to please others and to gain their approval (Kohlberg's third stage).

During adolescence two factors influence the questioning of rules and experimentation with alternative modes of behaviour. Firstly young people, as part of their quest for independence, need to test out and challenge the authority of parents and of those who exercise control over them. In this respect battles of will are little different from early childhood, except that the young man or woman has more weight, not only physically, but also in power of argument – for instance, the ability to use abstract thinking as described by Piaget starts in early adolescence. The second factor in questioning is the need to find a set of rules for oneself, accepted not because others say so, but because the rules have their own intrinsic validity. Out of this period of experimentation, which is sometimes only in mental or verbal argument, although sometimes also in action, a healthily maturing young person begins to discover her or his own identity and a set of values and ideas of what is right and wrong, and of what is important and what is peripheral in the corpus of tradition that has been taught by word and example since childhood. These values and ideas are not necessarily any different in content to parental and community standards, but radically different in the mature young person, because they are now based upon self-discovery rather than upon the need to conform to or rebel against the wishes of others. This is Kohlberg's fourth stage of moral development, which runs parallel to the finding of a personal identity in the Erikson model, that of personal recognition of the value of moral laws and social order.

Similarly, healthy questioning is part of the fourth stage of faith development, in the same way as the third stage in Fowler's model is linked to the conformity that I have described as present in the experience of learning in childhood. Conformity, of course, is also present in adolescence, where young people are heavily influenced by their peer group and by youth culture, to which they often conform slavishly. Finding individual identity slowly comes out of sharing in the common identity of an alternative sub-culture.

Yet many adults too are notoriously conformist, in their moral thinking, in their social expectations, and in their attitudes to faith; and rather than at this point pursue the sense of identity that can emerge after passing through a period of conformity (see next chapter), it is the conventional type of person I concentrate upon here. I include in this category some of those who attend churches as well as some of those who do not. Fowler calls his third stage of faith development 'Synthetic–Conventional',[15] and he believes that the majority of people, including those in congregations, belong to this category.[16] In this section, therefore, I am dealing with a crucial stage, which the majority of people reach, but much fewer move out of. Most pastoral care will be involved with people who are in this position in their development, even though in age, and in other aspects, they may have moved further through the Erikson stages into the making of intimate relationships, the bringing up of children, and progress in their work, and perhaps also in other areas of intellectual development. Even though our present European culture is largely critical of conventional religion, many people for much of the time (except perhaps for some in a crisis) hold 'anti-religious' or 'non-religious' views in a conventional way, which says more about their conformity to cultural norms than about their development towards new understandings of their search for faith.

Pastoral care, if it is to assist mature development, therefore needs to help people not only pass into but also out of the conformist stage. Unfortunately, pastoral care often gets stuck, as people themselves do, in the 'Synthetic-Conventional' stage, because communicating and absorbing the tradition of commandments and creeds (in addition to the stories that belong to earlier stages) becomes an end in itself, and not a means to more mature development. I do not wish to devalue this process of communication of tradition, nor to invalidate the appropriateness of enabling people initially to belong to a community (whether sacred or secular) by conforming to its expectations. Accepting conventions is probably an essential part both of joining a community, and of sharing in the enshrined wisdom of the community. This not only helps the community to accept a new member, but provides the new member with the raw materials from which, later on, more personal development can take place.

An analogy would be that it is essential at a certain stage of development to help children learn to read, and to write, and to acquire both basic information and simple logic, if they are to develop in their learning. But to expect the same type of learning in sixth-form colleges or in further or higher education would be to prevent young people learning how to question, or how to weigh and balance information, and from learning to generate new ideas and fresh interpretations. In the same way synthetic-conventional faith has value for a while, but the path towards maturity leads further on to the 'Individuative–Reflective' stage.

Fowler uses 'synthetic' in the sense that an individual draws upon other people's ways of thinking, but not in the sense that he or she tries to create a synthesis. He describes this type of faith as 'conventional', although recognizing that it takes account of a wider world and wider issues. In this stage faith provides a coherent orientation in the midst of a more complex world. It provides a sense of identity and outlook, although it is more a sense of common identity – like the adolescent finds security in his or her own sub-culture. As yet there is no real sense of autonomous judgement. In some ways, Fowler suggests, it is more like an ideology[17] than a personal faith, even though the beliefs may be very deeply held. Authority is still vested in traditional authority figures or in the valued peer group.

What is particularly valuable in Fowler's research is the way in which he demonstrates how some people hold such synthetic and conventional views, even when they are critical of religion and the Church. He quotes a middle-aged man, whose attitude that things are and always have been the same indicates a sense of being stuck. This applies as much to his faith:

> I'm not now a religious man, never was and never will be. Religion is just a lot of nonsense as I see it. As I see it, we are born, we live here, we die, and that's it. Religion gives people something to believe in, that there's something more, because they want there to be something more, but there isn't.[18]

I am aware that such statements might be interpreted as a thought-out opinion, and expressed more eloquently it could suggest a more individual reflective view. I think, however, that in this example Fowler is trying to convey the type of attitude which draws on what is thought to be 'common-sense' or conventional, popular wisdom. Faith, and criticism of the faith, can be equally conventional and dogmatic. Much depends upon the relationship between an individual's attitude and that of her or his sub-culture. In areas where it is the convention *not* to go to church, attitudes to the Church, and justification of certain positions, will often be conventionally critical, with equally conventional ideas about God: 'Of course, I believe in God, but you don't have to go to church to be a good Christian.' It requires not only courage but also a rare kind of individuality to break free from that type of conventional thinking. Likewise, within churches, there are sometimes similarly conventionally critical attitudes: 'You cannot really call yourself a Christian unless you come to church, or unless you believe in the Resurrection, or if you are a practising homosexual.' It often requires just as much courage, as well as that rare kind of individuality to remain within Christian communities, whilst at the same time to stand out over against those communities' most restrictive conventions, especially when the majority of a congregation is itself mainly composed of Christians at the synthetic–conventional stage.

I do not imply that the faith of this stage, or of the community of this stage, is simple and narrow. As we grow older, we discover that people and relationships become more complicated, and faith in God, where it is thought about, expands to include much more complex depths than had been thought before. Belief in God may involve a deeper sense of personal relationship with the transcendent. The personal qualities of God become more important than the physical attributes of a child's imagery. But because of the increasing complexity of the questions and thinking about God and other aspects of the faith, as well as questions about people and relationships and ethical issues, there is, not unnaturally, a need for a sense of order. Synthetic-conventional faith meets this need.

This stage bears a strong resemblance to Tillich's World-view B. World-view A, described in the previous chapter, often becomes inadequate as issues become more complex, and deeper questioning begins, sometimes initiated by others, sometimes from within oneself. Literalism wears thin at the edges, but because uncertainty cannot be sustained for long, the search for order means that thorough-going questioning is often repressed, using 'an acknowledged authority with sacred qualities like the Church or the Bible, to which one owes unconditional surrender'.[19] Whether or not the answer is correct, the very act of receiving an authoritative answer helps many people, at least temporarily, to feel secure and more at ease within themselves. World-view B, unlike World-view A, is rather more fragile, because questions may persist, and grow more intense; or the answers provided by authority may eventually cease to be satisfying.

Cupitt alludes to the need for order when he describes doctrinal and metaphysical realism,[20] where religious thought is part of an ordered system, that is seen in the setting out of beliefs in authoritatively stated and ordered creeds, or in the need for ordered sequences such as the five pillars of faith, the ten commandments, the eight-fold path. The passion for order leads to certain contradictions: the trinitarian formula of three persons in one God, or the two natures of Christ, wholly man and wholly God. The contradictions have to be explained rationally. The wish for order, in some of our churches, has also led to a hierarchical method of church order, a pyramidical structure, which reflects the theological idea of orders of being. The reader may now understand my cautions earlier about taking the models of human development as being cut and dried, since I would not wish psychological descriptions to lose their value through being trapped in an over-rigid and over-ordered system!

The passion for order leads to certain problems. Some people think that faith can be argued, and either that the person who does not believe the same as they do is being unreasonable, or that the person who does not reason as they do is unbelieving. Reason and conviction are confused. Others use the power that comes with the ordering of institutions to punish or expel those who do not conform. Beliefs are treated like laws.[21] Obsessional behaviour is seen in some religious practices and ritual, where failure to comply with 'the way things have always been done' can lead to intense guilt and anxiety. Unquestioning obedience might be required by a church or a community, as in the worst kind of strict childhood. Symbols are sacred, and attempts to demythologize them are felt to be threatening to the symbol – to destroy its value in the very act of questioning it, as though the baby is being thrown out with the bath water.

Just as Erikson suggests that the ritual excess of the anal stage is legalism,[22] so too Faber[23] illustrates the dangers of conformist religion and thinking by reference to Freud's anal stage of development and to its equivalent in religious terms. Since it is in this stage of development that the issues of authority and autonomy are first encountered, this particular link is useful. He isolates three examples of anal religion. The first is phariseeism, where there was, according to the gospels, an obsessional mentality which insisted on dotting the i's and crossing the t's, where it appeared that man was made for the sabbath, and not the sabbath for man, where cleanliness laws were rigorously adhered to, where law was more important than liberty, and where 'you must' and 'you must not' seemed to be key words. The second form of anal religion is puritanism with its stress on status, on duty, on making money (without being seen to be spending it), on frugality and industry, on achievement, and good works, as ways of proving to oneself and others that salvation has been achieved and that one is a member of the predestined elect. In both phariseeism and puritanism, there is a sense in which religion appears not only to force religious believers into a straightjacket of rules, but also to bring the Almighty under the control of religion.

Faber also includes secularization as the third example of anal religion, although, unlike the other two which emphasize authority, this gives the wrong kind of weight to autonomy. With the advance of secularization, the emphasis in society is on achievement, on status, on making money, on ownership, and on the value of work. The manager has become a central figure. While it is not easy to call secularization itself a religion, the effect of secularization on people's values and sense of meaning has much in common with the phariseeism and puritanism which Faber puts alongside it, emphasizing doing and having rather than being.

The decline of religious belief has led to a new kind of belief, which lays excessive stress on humankind's autonomy. It is similar to one possible outcome of the period of adolescence, where a young person cuts himself from his roots, rather than finding individual identity alongside respect for his parents and his tradition. The increasing control of natural resources and forces has led to considerable weakening of the sense of being an equal part of creation, and to false inflation of humankind's ability to play at being God. As a defence against the anxiety of realizing our own finiteness and infinitively small place in the cosmos, we have deluded ourselves about our self-sufficiency. Faber gives the coronary patient as an example of the controlled and controlling individual, who shows every sign of anal characteristics. Perhaps the equivalent of the heart-attack to humankind is the impact of a natural or a man-made disaster, which temporarily brings us back to a realization that we are not gods. True autonomy does not preclude the necessity of belonging.

I am not certain that it is possible to follow Faber completely in isolating phariseeism and puritanism, as if they were separate religions, from Judaism, Islam and Christianity, which he places on a different, higher level. Phariseeism, puritanism, and even secularization themselves started as attempts to break away from other types of sterile conformity. Initially they were themselves attempts to find a new way. There is always the risk that any form of new thinking, within and outside the major religions, becomes both an '-ism', and a new way of forcing people into conformity. All movements have tendencies towards authoritarianism, and religious groups or ideas are no exceptions. As an idea grows, and a community forms around it, what started as a breakaway movement from slavish conformity can turn, within a short space of time into an ideology, which Fowler believes stage 3 faith easily becomes. Furthermore, the community, particularly if it stays closed and is preoccupied with defending its ideas from attack or criticism from outside as well as within, often fails to see itself as others see it, and loses touch with the way other people are thinking.

I may have dwelt overlong on some of the problems that arise from conformity, when it is my intention to concentrate on growth rather than on the psychopathology of individuals or institutions. Yet this is the most crucial area of pastoral care, because it is difficult for people to see conforming (or, as they might call it more positively, belonging) as a transitional phase rather than as an end in itself. Unfortunately for churches and religious groupings, in many ways institutions work best when they are constituted of a large group of stage 3 conventional people. As they are encouraged to grow in their search for autonomy and meaning, it is less easy for them to belong to a group of like-minded individuals. One of the outcomes of pastoral care which fosters more mature thinking and attitudes is that it will encourage people to question. At the same time there is a risk in that in doing this some of those who question may find it impossible to stay within a community, if the majority resist greater autonomy. Fortunately there are communities of faith, which Fowler would describe as stage 4 or 5 communities, where questioning is not seen as the unwelcome intrusion of unbelievers or of the devil, but in which it is recognized that it is part of the normal development of thinking and of faith. In these instances the question is how far such communities will allow the questioning and rethinking to go? Fowler suggests that stage 5 communities (which I guess are very rare) have, like stage 5 persons, 'the capacity to understand and relate to Christians of each of the other stages' as well as 'the religious traditions of others as strangers'.[24]

The tendency therefore is for the synthetic–conventional stage of faith development, like the anal stage of personality development, to be one in which people become *obsessed* with issues of authority and order, and with the linked concomitants of sin and of guilt. (I look at these last two key subjects in a more positive way in the next chapter, since in later stages I believe they can be freed from the excess of legalism.) Eric Fromm[25] described this obsession in his distinction between authoritarian and humanistic religion, the former clearly emerging from fixation of development at this stage, the latter more typical of later forms of maturity. Authoritarian religion emphasizes that humankind is *controlled* by a higher and external power, which is *entitled* to worship, obedience and reverence by very virtue of the fact that it has control. The italicized words are necessary to understand Fromm's position, which is not anti-theistic. His concern about this type of theism or about some non-theistic political beliefs is that obedience is stressed above the two principles of love and justice. 'The prevailing mood of authoritarian religion is that of sorrow and of guilt.'

Humanistic religions, amongst which Fromm included early Buddhism, the teachings of Isaiah and Jesus, and certain aspects of Judaism and Christianity, are distinguished by understanding 'God as a symbol of *man's own powers* which he tries to realize in his life, and not a symbol of force and domination, having *power over man* . . . God is the image of man's higher self, a symbol of what man potentially is or ought to become' (Fromm's italics). Pointing forward to themes I introduce in the next chapter, Fromm also writes: 'Faith is certainty of conviction based on one's own experience of thought and feeling, not assent to propositions on credit of the proposer.'

It may be valuable to add that, although Fromm paints a picture of people as powerless when in the grip of authoritarian religion, he observes that those who are the leaders and proponents of this type of religion often themselves exercise great power over their followers. This is relevant to pastoral care, because the exercise of power can just as easily be thrust upon pastors by those who are looking to them for strong leadership and authoritative guidance with their questions about faith and morals, and about their understanding of themselves in relation to their life and work. It is completely appropriate that at a certain stage of development, individuals and congregations should value and benefit from solid teaching, since this helps them to comprehend their faith and tradition more fully and so achieve that sense of 'coming together' and 'belonging' which has been positively described in this chapter. For the pastor this can be a rewarding ministry, when questions excite people's curiosity and when they hunger for knowledge. Unfortunately, some people want this knowledge either to bolster themselves against what could be important periods of doubt, or to find some way of achieving power over those who ask questions of their faith. They would sooner expound their own (or the Church's or the Bible's) answers, than listen to the outsider's search for understanding.

In pastoral care, therefore, pastors need to be wary of the way in which the educational process can replace ignorance with rigid and inflexible knowledge. Important though it is to enable those who wish it, to learn more about the Bible and the Church (for instance, in preparation for confirmation or church membership), some may seize upon information and apparent factual knowledge as a buttress against the anxieties that come from trying to sustain their faith, while living in a questioning and critical society.

Pastors are often treated, whether or not they see themselves as authoritative, as oracles of wisdom, whose words (as long as they say what people expect to hear) are swallowed unquestioningly. Should they say those things which conventional people do not want to hear, their words will be quietly or stormily dismissed. The pastor also needs to bear in mind that some people will resist deeper questioning, because of their fear of appearing to contradict authority, and others because they are afraid of the void that may result from asking too many questions.

It is not possible, however impatient the stage 4 person often feels with stage 3 faith, to hasten the period of deeper questioning that sometimes follows initial satisfaction with straightforward factual answers. Since many pastors find themselves working with people (inside and outside the Church) who are in this stage of synthetic-conventional faith, they may be able to prepare the way for greater autonomy and for freedom from authoritarian attitudes. This can be done firstly (as Fowler suggests[26]) by regularly speaking of faith, like life itself, as a journey, where changes are to be expected, although they will happen for different people at different times and at a different pace. Encouragement can be gently imparted for people to look further, and not to imagine that they have ever 'arrived'. Secondly, the pastor can prepare people to be aware that crises are also opportunities,[27] and that for most people crises are inevitable. It is often through crises that personal growth, including development of faith, occurs. Thirdly, a pastor can prepare people for greater autonomy by personally avoiding dogmatic statements; by stressing the fluidity and openness to change of her or his own opinions; by using expressions in teaching, preaching and personal conversations that emphasize the different ways of looking at issues that are open to people, both within the traditions of the Church as well as outside it; and by learning to speak without being afraid to use qualifying statements, such as 'perhaps', 'we cannot be sure', etc. Fourthly, a pastor can demonstrate the value that comes from people sharing differences, rather than from maintaining a falsely secure unity, based upon fear of conflict. Finally, a pastor who provides what was referred to earlier as a 'facilitating environment', can listen in people for the first signs of a developing identity and more individual reflections, encouraging as healthy the specific questions and views which people share. He or she can affirm, where there is doubt about the expression of such opinions, that growing towards the fullness of Christ often involves taking new directions and stepping, cautiously or boldly, into unknown territory.

Needless to say, with so many people in this conventional stage none of these approaches are easy, because the pastor, whatever her or his stage of personal growth, often feels trapped by strong group pressures. A pastor is not unnaturally anxious about incurring the wrath of those who are most defensive, and may sometimes be forced back to questioning whether or not her or his own steps towards maturity have been, or still are, on the right path. I have met clergy who are afraid to share their thinking with lay people, lest they be decried for their views. I have also met many lay people who are afraid to share their doubts, lest they offend their pastor. It is surprising what relief there is when two such people get together! I may have painted an over-pessimistic picture of some congregations and done them an injustice, because there is a much more positive side. The encouragement which pastors give to people to integrate 'I believe' statements with the 'We believe . . .' tradition of the Church can also bring a breath of fresh air to those, inside and outside congregations, who silently, sometimes rather guiltily, wait for permission to grow.

1. J. W. Fowler, *Stages of Faith: the Psychology of Human Development and the Quest for Meaning* (San Francisco, Harper and Row, 1981), ch. 17.
2. ibid., chs. 15 and 16.
3. A. Freud, *Normality and Pathology in Childhood* (Penguin 1973), pp. 64–76.
4. H. Guntrip, *Psychoanalytic Theory, Therapy and the Self* (Hogarth Press 1971), p. 42.
5. E. Erikson, *Childhood and Society* (Penguin 1965), ch. 8.
6. Fowler, *Stages of Faith*, p. 149.
7. ibid., p. 127.
8. ibid., p. 138.

9. ibid., p. 128.
10. R. Goldman, *Readiness for Religion* (Routledge and Kegan Paul 1965), p. 17.
11. D. Cupitt, *Life Lines* (SCM Press 1986), ch. 2.
12. ibid., p. 34.
13. W. E. Baldridge and J. J. Gleason, 'A Theological Framework for Pastoral Care' (*The Journal of Pastoral Care*, xxxii, 4, 1978), p. 237.
14. Fowler, *Stages of Faith*, p. 149.
15. ibid., pp. 151–73.
16. ibid., p. 161; J. W. Fowler, *Faith Development and Pastoral Care* (Fortress Press 1987), p. 87. See also B. Reed, *The Dynamics of Religion* (Darton Longman and Todd 1978), where the psychology of group dynamics adds considerably to our understanding of congregations.
17. Fowler, *Stages of Faith*, p. 173.
18. ibid., p. 166.
19. Quoted by Baldridge and Gleason. op. cit., p. 234.
20. Cupitt. op. cit., chs. 3 and 4.
21. ibid., pp. 39–40.
22. See D. Capps, *Life Cycle Theory and Pastoral Care* (Fortress Press 1983), pp. 61–3.
23. H. Faber, *Psychology of Religion* (SCM Press 1972).
24. Fowler, *Faith Development and Pastoral Care*, p. 94.
25. The following paragraph and quotations draw upon: E. Fromm, *Psychoanalysis and Religion* (Yale University Press 1967), pp. 32–51.
26. Fowler, *Faith Development and Pastoral Care*, pp. 116–7. See also ch. 1, note 12, for other references to 'the journey'.
27. ibid., pp. 102–3.

6

Diversities

Taking Bearings

Since the path that development towards maturity takes is far from straightforward, it might be helpful to pause a moment, to take our bearings, and look both back at where the last two chapters have brought us and forward to where the next two chapters will take us. Growth takes place in a number of ways, all of which contribute to the whole person. Some features consist of major developmental tasks which almost invariably have to be faced. These are brought about firstly through the natural processes of physical growth and ageing, over which we have little control, and to which we constantly have to adapt; and secondly through various expectations or requirements such as attendance at school between certain ages, or the age of retirement, as well as social expectations such as marriage by a certain age, having children, and later letting go of responsibilities in favour of younger people, although this is balanced in some societies by the value attached to the wisdom of the old.

In addition to these developments, which have a certain inevitability about them, there are others which may or may not take place, depending upon the stimulation given to us by family, education and opportunity, such as the development of capacities of thought and reflection, which, together with life circumstances, may lead to increasing maturity in conceptual thinking, in moral thinking and decision-making, and in the search for meaning. These rather more fluid developments sometimes stop short of full development, not necessarily disadvantaging a person, although perhaps making this side of life less rich; whereas those tasks described above have to be faced, even if they are not always resolved satisfactorily.

These different types of development do not move forward in synchronization. One form may outstrip another, although, in the attempt to summarize and simplify, these chapters put together similar stages of maturity in all the main fields that have been introduced.

It is possible, therefore, for a sixty-year-old person to be at a stage 3 (Kohlberg and Fowler) stage of moral thinking and faith development, whereas his or her physical and ego development (i.e. Erikson's model) has reached the stage of old-age issues of integrity versus despair. The type of moral thinking and faith which that person has, particularly whether they are basically positive or negative, will no doubt influence the way in which the basic issues of the final stage of life are resolved.

On the other hand, a younger person in mid-thirties, who has had a number of semi-committed relationships but who gains satisfaction in his or her work as a teacher, may show some aspects of the creativity stage (Erikson's 'Middle Adulthood'), though stop short in close relationships of the commitment to intimacy which would be expected of someone who had resolved Erikson's 'Young Adulthood' stage. Yet his or her moral thinking may be stage 5 (Kohlberg) and faith development at stage 4 (Fowler). Again, we see different levels of maturity.

Or we can imagine a twenty-year-old student, who is physically mature and at the peak of physical fitness, whose intellectual capacity is such that he or she can work in the higher realms of conceptual thinking (for example, pure mathematics), but whose moral thinking is still based on a mixture of fear and pleasing others, who is unable to make relationships with other people except through membership of the local church, and whose faith is literal and conventional. Here physical and intellectual maturity run far ahead of the altogether much more restricted development of other areas of his or her life.

These many layers of development are well illustrated by Figure 8 (p. 40). Pastoral care of the whole person has to take account not simply of body and mind but also of moral and faith development, as well as of emotional and interpersonal levels of maturity. Because in many people these layers are at different stages, and yet also bear upon one another, it is a complex task to both identify where, at any one time, a person is, and in which direction they could most beneficially be encouraged to move.

As if this were not enough, I particularly wish in this chapter to draw out another feature of development, which is a slow but continual swing between being an individual and being in relationship to others, which weaves its way through the stages in what is (fortunately) a regular pattern. Perhaps I can best start by considering in more detail, using the analogy of a long walk across country, the symbol of the journey.

A traveller walking alone across a certain terrain sees, in the misty distance, the outline of what appears a craggy hill, but it is far from clear. As the traveller slowly approaches the hill, the outline takes on different shapes and meanings: at one time in the traveller's eyes it looks like a huge granite rock, which in imagination takes the form of all manner of fantastic creatures. At another point it becomes clearer, as a building on a hill, but that building is still not clear. Is it a castle, or is it an even more ancient monument The traveller at this distance can only interpret what the eyes see through imagination and phantasy.

As the walker gets nearer, and catches up with a band of ramblers, there is an opportunity for companionship on the way. They have a map, and several of them know about different aspects of the landmark ahead. It is marked on the map as an old monastery, and various fellow-travellers tell our walker about the style of building, the life of the order that used to live there, the lives of some of the more famous monks, the history of the decline of the order, and so on. Our traveller eagerly absorbs the information, moving from imagination and myth to greater reality, at the same time seeing the distant hill in a clearer light; his (or her) eyes (assisted by what he has now been told) can make out the shapes. The company is pleasant, the party stops at places along the way, and the traveller listens to the tales, and falls in with the customs of the group.

As they proceed, the traveller begins to feel restless. There is a certain 'know it all' quality to the companions, and they make it clear that their journey takes them a mile or two out of the way of the monastery on the hill. The traveller wants to take a closer look, and so he (or she) leaves the group to take its chosen route, and sets out, once more alone. As the ground rises, and the ruins come into focus, the walker realizes that some of what the fellow walkers said was true – the architecture is indeed late gothic, the size and layout of the building indicates that it was such and such a community. But in other respects the ramblers had got some details wrong, since they had gone on what they had been told, and had not fully explored the site for themselves. The traveller is nonetheless fascinated, goes back to the nearest village for the night, and returns the next day, seeing the building in a new light. Each time our walker approaches the hill by different paths, and sees new dimensions every time. Understanding and vision broaden.

The traveller stays for some time in the locality, and meets other individuals, who also visit the hill and its ruins. They talk with each other. They share the way they see things, and sometimes they disagree about interpretations both of the facts about the place, and sometimes about the way they see it. But they also learn from each other, never trying to convince the other, but rather mutually exploring the subject and discovering that it is capable of myriad understandings. They realize that even if they stayed there for weeks, the hill and its ruins would always have new secrets to reveal.

This analogy of another line of development shows the movement between perceiving for oneself, and perceiving through and with the help of others. A child starts life, as a tiny baby, apparently as an individual, although, as I explained in chapter 4, bound up unawares in a relationship between self and another person, who is not yet experienced as a separate being. First perceptions are highly idiosyncratic, little informed by awareness of reality, and interpreted in all sorts of fantastic ways. During early infancy a child begins to attain independence, but at the same time begins to make sense of experience through what others say, as well as through his or her own perceptions. From the individuality of early childhood, he or she moves into relationships with other children, with other adults, and in peer groups, learning from them, and fitting in with their conventions and customs, because it feels more secure to belong than to be separate. For some at the stage of adolescence, and for others around mid-life (Fowler suggests it is often a crisis which precipitates it), there can be a breaking away from conventional views, and the beginning of a journey of discovery for oneself. This is again highly individualistic and resembles the working out of personal identity in gender, role and work terms. Although this individual stance may remain as a fairly fixed position, some continue to explore and begin to seek out the company of others who are engaged in a similar quest. These others are valued not because of the clear answers they give to questions, nor for the security of holding common opinions, but because they provide other perspectives. Yet awareness grows that the quest for understanding is, in more than one sense, beyond them all.

This ebb and flow is not surprising since it is also reflected in the way individuals generally move throughout life between dependence and independence with periods, especially in mature development, of interdependence. Being alone, and being with others is a movement present throughout early life, from moving away from the dependence of infancy to the greater independence of childhood; from the breaking away from home as an adolescent to the dependence on peers, and in the same period breaking free from dependence on the peer group to what is often, especially initially, a dependent relationship in marriage. As the children of a marriage leave home, a couple (together or sometimes separately) face a new period of independence, and the ageing process in turn brings independence from work, although ageing frequently involves increasing dependence upon others.

In chapter 4 I showed how the child perceived the world, self, and faith in idiosyncratic ways. I looked in the last chapter at more unified understanding, and more realistic perceptions, coming through the influence of family, school and other groups, together with a greater intellectual ability to grasp different dimensions. In the sections that follow I show how the period of belonging gives way to a search for greater identity or individuality. Yet even this next stage is not an end in itself, but another step towards the fullness of

Christ. In the final section of this chapter I move to the point where a person looks deeper than conscious reasoning, and discovers new depths to individuality; and to the point where new-found individuality discerns that it is impossible to be complete without other people. So a person is drawn back again to being with others, and sometimes beyond this to a deeper sense of belonging to creation as a whole. This is the point of development towards which this chapter reaches.

Achieving Identity

There is a close parallel between the developmental task (according to the Erikson model) of achieving sufficient personal identity in order to engage in an intimate relationship ('being together but being separate'[1]), and stage 4 in the Fowler model, Individuative–Reflective faith,[2] although the two are rarely coterminous chronologically. In both models this stage is characterized by a breaking away from assumed systems of values and belief. While it is possible that values and meaning *may* not change dramatically, it is during this stage that what has previously been accepted as a tacit set of values now becomes more explicit. Ideas are more thought through, and no longer accepted simply because others say so. Identity, in the stage 4 person, is no longer derived simply from a sense of belonging, but from the first signs of self-knowledge which, we shall see, goes even further in Fowler's stage 5.

This breaking away has what Freudians would call an oedipal quality to it. In the oedipal stage of development a child needs to dissolve the intensity of the relationship to his or her parents by *beginning* to make a move away from them. This usually and quite normally comes to a head in adolescence, when in a metaphorical sense parents have to be prepared to be 'killed off'. Winnicott deliberately used such evocative imagery when he wrote: 'If the child is to become an adult then this move is achieved over the dead body of an adult . . . where there is the challenge of a growing boy or girl, there let an adult meet the challenge. And it will not necessarily be nice.'[3] It is also necessary for an adult to survive this challenge, to be 'killed off' and yet to rise again. Where a parent can go through this process with her or his growing children, adult-to-adult relationships can be built with them, based (after the stormy period of adolescent testing of boundaries) on mutual respect. The mythology of the dying and rising god is obviously pertinent to this stage of development.

In considering these aspects, it needs to be borne in mind that pastoral care also has to be prepared to meet such healthy challenges. The pastor or the church may, for a time, have to be 'killed off' (and yet to survive) if people are to be allowed to discover the value and the authority of their own experience and search for understanding. Just as adolescence is often a stressful time for parents and teenagers, so discovery of personal identity in terms of faith raises dilemmas for pastoral care. In the interests of more mature faith, it may be essential for the Church and for conventional faith to be 'sacrificed', and for people to move away into their own desert experience. Leaving the Church, even temporarily, is no soft option, and may involve more suffering and pain than staying within it. But can (or should) people be encouraged to do this? Or, as 'with-it' parents may prevent adolescents from testing boundaries, would such 'permission' invalidate the necessary and self-directed spontaneity of breaking away, and impoverish the value of the struggle with authority. How can young people (and adults at the right stage of development) be permitted to be 'immature', as Winnicott suggests they should, without the parent church at the same time being seen to be abdicating responsibility? How can pastoral care help those who need to break away to resume later a good relationship with a church which is discovered, like their parents, to be a little less authoritarian and a little wiser than they thought! And how can clergy, who often themselves need to make this break, at least for a while, be helped to do so, when so much hangs upon such a decision? I have no answers, but it is important to raise the questions.

A genuine move to this stage of development means interrupting the reliance on external authority-figures or groups. Authority is relocated within the self, although others remain important to provide counsel and advice, and to share their own expectations. This move away from the previous relatively secure stage of conformity, is typified by a number of tensions, which Faber includes under an earlier phase: the dialectic between activity and passivity, between independence and dependence, and between defiance, and shame and doubt.[4] Fowler describes similar tensions in stage 4, between being an individual and being defined by group membership; between subjectivity and the power of strong but unexamined feelings on the one hand, and objectivity and critical reflection on the other; between self-fulfilment, and service to and concern for others.

Writing of religious movements, Faber's main treatment of this stage comes in his chapters on the adolescent phase.[5] He refers there to a phase of religion itself, and not to faith as experienced in adolescence. He describes our current age as one of inner disorganization, of attempts at integration, of forming a life-plan, of finding identity and a place in the world, of searching for identification and identity, of experimenting with the 'primal themes of human existence', of the fading of the hierarchical structures, of more open rebellion against authoritarianism, and of the formation of new ideologies. The adolescent phase of religion, he writes, changes the concept of order, and moves more in the direction of the dispersion experience. Jesus, far from being a symbol of traditional authority and power, is now seen as a revolutionary figure, similar to those in the counter-culture of youth.[6] Like Bonhoeffer, Faber sees mankind as come of age, and he describes the adolescent phase of religion as the point which we have now reached. Unfortunately, stopping short at the adolescence stage as he does in his study, he makes only passing reference to later developments, such as the experience of other faiths, which different authors have taken further.

Faber's picture is a hopeful one, but not easily recognizable in conventional Western society. There may have been breaking away from the Church, but often it is replaced by the adoption of an equally conventional secular value system. Fowler requires more for stage 4 development, including the ability to shape one's own variant way of living. This is a bold step to take, because cutting loose means a serious move into the unknown, although Fowler suggests that whether a person can genuinely make such a move depends upon the character and quality of those alternative groups which the person may join – in other words, there is still some need for group identity.[7] In some congregations there may be small groups which provide the right milieu; although the climate for more Individuative-Reflective faith is often more bracing in the secular world, in universities, and in the serious treatment of religious questions by the media. Of course there are always some people who follow even the latest intellectual fashion without thinking it through for themselves. The parallel in psychological terms, as Fowler points out, drawing I imagine upon Erikson, is the adolescent who enters into a marital relationship too soon in order to avoid the challenges of 'individuative transition'.[8] Distinguishing between the person who is personally wrestling with issues, and the person who has conformed to the latest intellectual convention may call for some discrimination in the pastoral conversation.

Nurturing individual identity in pastoral care means recognizing and respecting differences, which stretches more than tolerance. It provides the opportunity for widening understanding. Indeed in this stage clear delineation of differences is often more important than the recognition of what is held in common, which is found in Fowler's stage 5. Stage 4 faith is paralleled in the need to find sexual and gender identity, and to find identity through work. (Vocation is another subject which has engaged Fowler's interest.[9]) In pastoral care, recognition of individual identity includes understanding gender issues. Feminist psychology is just beginning to show us (particularly us men!) that gender differences give rise to divergent paths of personality development well before the genital stage, where Freud and many of his followers believed divergence began.

Much as it would be valuable to explore some of those differences here, the risk of inadequately summarizing such thinking suggests this is an area which needs to be followed through elsewhere.[10] More immediately relevant for pastoral care is the possibility that men and women may have different perceptions of faith, just as Gilligan[11] has suggested there may be differences between the way men and women approach moral problems. Faber asks whether there is a different experience of God in men and women? The correlation between images of parents and the image of God, which I introduced in chapter 4, is extended in research to which Faber[12] refers, where the influence of the mother image on the psychological attitude to God is more frequently and strongly felt by men and boys, and of the father image by women and girls. In another research[13] enquiry it was found that the idea of God in adolescent boys was more strongly marked by the concept of the 'Holy Virgin' than by Christ, although the opposite was true in girls. Both these pieces of research took place in European Catholic cultures, and may have less significance in the Anglo-Saxon milieu!

The nature of diversity is that it confronts conventionality with a wide range of startling options. The need to find identity is often initially accompanied by a passionate and single-minded assertion of separateness. It is to be expected that groups which are finding a voice, and asserting their identity, should sometimes appear hostile to anyone who is not one of them. Diversity and individuality may provide a real test for pastoral ministry, as it is forced to come to terms with the assertion of identity by blacks, feminists, gay men and lesbians, as well with radical questioning of faith and order, and of moral positions. Similarly, the range of forms which theological thinking may take in Individuative-Reflective faith is glimpsed in the options that emerge from Cupitt's 'Metro map'.[14] Although it is unnecessary to list his definitions here, many of them emerged, as we might expect of stage 4 expressions of faith, from the 'oedipal/adolescent' overthrow of authoritarian religion following the Reformation and the Enlightenment. He also includes forms of religious consciousness which tie in with Tillich's World-view C, and with Conjunctive Faith, Fowler's stage 5.

Important though this stage is, I suspect that it tends towards reductionism, and towards narrow explanation. Finding and defending one's own position takes priority over interest in and understanding of others' beliefs. Whereas a person in stage 5 is likely to be understanding of those who are still in earlier stages of development, stage 4 people, like those in the formative years of late adolescence and early adulthood, are often more radical and impatient. However, their radicalism can find positive expression in their concern about social issues and the rights of others, which is also seen in Kohlberg's stages 4 and 5 of moral development.

In this stage of development, demythologization often takes place, but the main interest is in what symbols and myths mean, and how they can be translated into propositions and definitions. In Tillich's terms, symbols are 'broken', but perhaps not yet recognized as pointing beyond themselves. As defined by Baldridge and Gleason[15], Tillich's World-view C person has reached beyond the Fowler stage 4 and into stage 5; hence the question mark I insert in Figure 8 between World-views B and C, indicating a stage of questioning prior to new use of the broken myth and symbol. Fowler states that the questioning stage 4 person begins to have some sense of initiative over the symbol, although at first the translation of meanings of symbols into concepts can also lead to a sense of loss, grief or even guilt. For example, the symbols and myths about eternal life may become in the end impossible to sustain intellectually. To let go of those myths is not just to experience some guilt in overthrowing one's Christian tradition; it is also to experience the anxiety that perhaps (and all we can say is perhaps) there is nothing more. The pain of the cross, which some 'conventional stage' Christians talk about as if it only applied to those who hold the 'true faith', might be just as real to those who struggle to find both themselves and a new relationship with a God whose former meaning has forsaken them. Stage 5, which has its own anguish, at least provides evidence that myths and symbols, once broken, can take new life.

Fowler observes that stage 4 can lead also to excessive confidence in the conscious mind and in critical thought, and so to a kind of second narcissism. Erikson described the 'ritual excess' of this stage as elitism, which is a similar notion, although expressed in group terms. In fact people may become stuck in this phase, not recognizing that life is more complex than stage 4's emphasis on clear distinctions and abstract concepts. There may, for instance, be some liberation of sexuality, but not without nigglings of guilt, as though liberation was more an attempt to overthrow authority (unsuccessful in some respects inasmuch as it does not adequately deal with the internal authority which continues to needle) than to find sexual pleasure. Stage 4 carries the risk with it of throwing the baby out with the bathwater. A good illustration of the effect of this stage on a group of Catholic undergraduates in the 1950s can be found in David Lodge's novel *How Far Can You Go*?.[16]

In fact, although I have throughout this section drawn the parallel with the adolescent search for identity, the transition to stage 4 (where it occurs at all) does not occur for some adults until their thirties or forties, often following a change in primary relationships, or a move, or the experience of a breakdown.[17] Such crises challenge the inadequacy of synthetic-conventional faith. The upheaval that such events cause may involve a long transition of several years. Likewise there is a transition out of stage 4, already referred to above, and explained more fully below, towards a broader and more open quest for truth and understanding.

Individuation and Conjunctive Faith

Individuation is a Jungian term, which does not carry the same meaning as Fowler's word 'Individuative' used of his stage 4. Jung's description of the psychological task of the second half of life much more appropriately links with this next stage of development, because stage 5 in Fowler's scheme, which he calls Conjunctive Faith,[18] is unusual before mid-life. It involves a more complex way of looking at faith, moving beyond the either/or of stage 4, into seeing many sides of an issue simultaneously. It is a stage when people look for patterns and inter-relatedness, but not by forcing everything into their own mind-set. Experience, including experience of symbols, is allowed to impinge upon a person.

There is an air of certainty, at least once the process has been established, that accompanies the breaking of the symbol in stage 4, which is unlike the way in which the symbol is used in stage 5, and which leads altogether in a different direction. Stage 4 leads to a new sense of order, but stage 5 exposes a person to the risk of uncertainty again. For a person to question something they have always held to be true, as in stage 4, requires some courage. It may mean that some symbols can never be the same again. But the stage 5 person moves beyond this dilemma, into a frame of mind where, as

Keats describes, defining the term 'negative capability': 'a man is capable of being in uncertainties, mysteries, doubts, without any irritable reaching after fact and reason'.[19] Nevertheless, Tillich assumes that World-view C people still feel anxious: although at the same time they are more positive about the value of anxiety than World-view B people. Their uncertainty cannot be relieved by World-view A natural literalism, or by World-view B's sacred authority. Courage is needed to be in stage 5, of which Tillich writes: 'Courage does not need the safety of unquestionable conviction. It includes the risk without which no creative life is possible.'[20]

Tillich's World-view C involves the broken symbol, that 'points beyond itself . . . participates in that to which it points . . . opens up levels of reality which otherwise are closed . . . unlocks dimensions and elements of our soul which correspond to the dimensions and elements of reality (opened up by myth or symbol) . . . and grows out of the individual or collective unconscious'. As Baldridge and Gleason add, 'Nothing but a myth or symbol is able to express the ultimate.'[21]

By being willing to suspend reason temporarily, people can enjoy symbols and phantasy, not as an escape, but as a way of learning and or returning to the reality of daily life enriched by the inward journey. (I referred to the value of this in worship on p. 70.) There are therefore even deeper gains for the stage 5 person than for the stage 4 person, whose rather more limited interpretation of the meaning of symbols to some extent also leads to the experience of new dimensions. Rayner[22] suggests that overcoming the denial of mortality can be a relief, and can enrich life, and I suspect the same is true of symbols. It may in the end be a relief that the symbol does not have to be true in itself, and there may be relief in not having to keep up the pretence that it is. But by translating it into new and even deeper dimensions, the symbol acquires an even greater significance, especially when the symbol is allowed to speak for itself. Whereas stage 4 implies a certain control over symbols, stage 5 once more lets the symbol take control, but this time in an interplay (and the word 'play' may be very important here) between imagination and reason.

In terms already familiar to us from Winnicott, Pruyser[23]

suggests that transcendent objects are prefigured by a child's transitional objects. We live, he writes, in three worlds. The first is the world of inner subjective experience and the second is that of outer objective experience, but there is a third which is 'located between and beyond the other two'.[24] This is the sphere of the imaginative. The process of playing with 'illusions' lies at the heart of the visual arts, literature, sciences, religion and music, assisting both the journey of discovery, and human transcendence and transformation. Like Erikson, Pruyser goes beyond Freud's brief description of the aim of human life, 'to love and to work' and inserts the idea of play. Imagination and play constitute the third world, relating us to the transcendent and the universal.

Conjunctive faith is therefore open to new experience and to being taken by surprise. Being in this stage does not mean losing touch with one's own version of reality, or one's own tradition, but realizing that reality is also to be found elsewhere too. Yet even the new meanings discovered in this way are recognized as being 'relative, partial and inevitably distorting apprehensions of transcendent reality.'[25]

The relativity of religious traditions is now seen not so much in terms of how they compare and relate to each other – in a quasi-competitive way), but how they all relate to the 'reality' which they try to mediate and interpret. Sharing the insights of other faiths is therefore important, and a step beyond the recognition in stage 4 that other people can think differently. Complementarity replaces competition. In stage 5, people discover how others' ways of understanding can inform their own. The idea of 'passing over', which occurs in the writing of John Dunne,[26] illustrates how new perspectives arise from immersion in other faiths, before the journey back to one's own, now newly enriched by the experience and by another perspective.

Expressed in Jungian terms, symbols are expressions of universal archetypes of the collective unconscious, to be found as much in other religions and cultures as in our own. Put in Freudian terms, symbols, like dreams, are part of the 'royal road' to the personal unconscious. This leads to another element of this stage of life which needs to be considered. Fowler includes as a characteristic of Conjunctive Faith that a person has to come to terms with his or her own unconscious, and with the fact that reason and the conscious ego are not master or mistress of its own house. Conscious and unconscious need to be integrated. The recognition that reason cannot altogether be trusted, and that self-deception is a constant possiblity is of course a feature which unites both Freudian and Jungian approaches. The psychotherapeutic setting requires an 'outsider' (the therapist) to provide a more objective view.

The Freudian desire to make the unconscious conscious is little different from the Jungian concept of individuation, defined by Samuels as 'the movement towards wholeness by means of integration of conscious and unconscious parts of the personality'.[27] Although this process may be started in the first half of life, particularly if a person receives counselling or therapy, it is more likely to take place in an older client who takes their counselling or therapy on, beyond the immediate crisis, into longer-term psychotherapy, or into continuing self-analysis. Perhaps it is only with the experience of passing years that we recognize that change is not as straightforward as we imagined when younger, and that there is more going on within us than we cared to admit in the rationalizing days of youth. Older people may also be more prepared to be dependent on another's help (be it pastor, therapist or spiritual director) than a young person who takes pride in new found independence. We also, I suspect, take a long time to throw off the need to please internalized parents. There is a sense in which deeper working on self-understanding cannot take place with any honesty until we have ceased to feel so guilty about or ashamed of every error or fault we find in ourselves.

Fowler gives a useful illustration of the type of thinking I have in mind as belonging with this stage of development. Mrs T is asked about her understanding of sin. She replies, 'Sin? I don't use the word sin, *ever* . . . I think more in terms of mistakes than I do of deliberate sin . . . In my own life I would perhaps describe it more as blundering because I didn't have the experience to handle things right.'[28] Later in the interview she speaks of sin as being cut off from God, but also talks about stupidity rather than sin. In her simple words she expresses her ability to accept herself, to forgive herself, and also to learn from her experience.

I have deliberately not introduced sin and guilt before this point because I have been more interested in positive growth towards maturity than the type of psychopathology, in which sin and guilt are so often experienced as things to be got rid of. I do not want to give the impression that guilt is purely neurotic, nor that 'sin' is insignificant in healthy development. Guilt can lead to concern for others, and towards the reparation of broken relationships. In that sense it is both positive and constructive. But Kohlberg has shown how moral judgements are made in the early stages of development on the basis of fear, of bargaining, of pleasing or not pleasing others, and of conforming or not conforming to society's expectations. Guilt or shame in earlier development are often based much more upon concern for what others might think of me, than what I feel they may be experiencing as a result of my wrong actions. The need for forgiveness often takes the form of needing to be loved again, rather than making reparation to the person who has been offended. Guilt and condemnation can frequently be projected by scapegoating others, and by splitting off responsibility on to 'the devil in me' 'temptation', or even in popular and misunderstood Freudian terms, to 'my parents' fault.'

In a mere paragraph I can do little justice to these complex issues of sin and guilt, although it is important to observe that psychodynamic theory (whether Freudian, Jungian or Kleinian) makes at least as great, if not greater, demands upon us as traditional Christian thinking does about sin and forgiveness. Firstly, psychodynamic thinking requires that we accept that everything that happens to us also involves our responsibility, and that when we do wrong it comes from within us, and not from outside. Secondly, that when we do wrong, there is an important reason for it, which needs to be understood if we are to change unsatisfactory ways of thinking and behaving. Thirdly, psychodynamic thinking demonstrates how we employ all manner of defences to help us avoid facing the truth about ourselves; and lastly, that there is no sin, fault or neurotic trait which we see in other people that is not also somewhere (if sometimes deep) within ourselves.

If we have heard much of this before, it is, of course, in the 'mote and the beam'[29] and in other places in the Sermon on the Mount.

A mature way of dealing with guilt, I suggest, involves a number of aspects: firstly, careful discrimination between what *is* our own and what is *not* our own responsibility. We tend to overblame others or ourselves, finding it difficult to apportion responsibility appropriately. Secondly, I suggest mature guilt involves full ownership of all that is our responsibility; but without feeling so weighed down by the acceptance of responsibility that we are prevented from taking a third step. This is to accept that, when we do wrong, or react badly to a situation, old unhelpful patterns of thinking and behaving are still around. That they have broken through is a sign to us that there are experiences, feelings and thoughts from our past which still need to be understood, worked through, and (perhaps one day) left behind. Fourthly, mature guilt involves the wish to make reparation, where it is necessary, and where it is still possible, in an appropriate manner; mature reparation is more concerned for the person who has been hurt than it is for the self. And lastly, a mature attitude to guilt means that when it is impossible to make such reparation (when, for example, someone we have hurt has died or gone away), we can accept this without further guilt.

Fowler has been criticized for failing to pay enough attention to the unconscious, or to the distinction between ego and self, in his emphasis upon ego-psychology.[30] Sketchy though his references are, there is no doubt that he intends the recognition of the unconscious to be one of the developmental tasks of this stage of faith, and that he points beyond the limits of the ego to opening oneself up to the 'voices of one's "deeper self" '.[31] I am aware that I too can only give both these important topics brief attention, although I am sure that the widening vision of this age and stage includes constant reference both outwards, to the accumulated wisdom of other traditions, and also inwards, to the treasures (covered by an accumulation of debris and detritus though some of them are!) to be found in one's deeper self.

There is also a third type of widening vision, which particularly applies to those who have reached the Erikson stage of late adulthood, where the issues are of integrity versus despair. This applies to older men and women, whether or not they have entered the stage of Conjunctive Faith, where Fowler includes this third aspect. This wider vision involves looking back, over the years, reclaiming and reworking one's past. This is not a book about pastoral care of the elderly, but if it were, I would wish to stress the importance of listening to old people as they remember stories from their lives. Randall[32] says that reminiscing serves the function of holding together the fragmenting self. An old person is more aware of fragmentation than younger, more active people, because there are more bodily and emotional changes than there have been since infancy and adolescence to disturb feelings of self-cohesion. Self-cohesion and self-esteem in the elderly person is sorely tried, and the act of reminiscing is a means of trying to maintain a sense of self.

This stage may seem to express the pinnacle of personal and faith development; but Fowler says that one of the dangers of this stage is that it can lead to paralyzing passivity and inaction, to complacency or cynical withdrawal, as if accepting the paradoxical nature of truth means that there is little point in doing anything. (I assume here he does not include the elderly whose passivity has a different, more physical explanation.) Because there is a basic division in the experience of this stage, between seeing the vision of a transformed world, but also apprehending that the world is untransformed, the temptation is to think that nothing can be done about it. If there is any loss from moving from stage 4 into stage 5 it can sometimes be that concern for others is not always translated so enthusiastically into action. Fowler therefore supposes a stage 6, where this division between vision and reality yields to what he calls 'radical actualization'.

Given that Fowler (like myself) writes in mid-life, and without therefore the actual experience of more mature years, it is scarcely surprising that there appears some confusion in him about the precise demarcation between stages 5 and 6. Though he feared that stage 5 did not exist,[33] he now clearly believes it does. Neither by age nor experience do I have anything more positive to offer, but I have my own doubts about reserving the translation of vision into action for stage 6. It is easier to see stage 5 as capable of either a purely contemplative, or a more active expression. Indeed, I am uncertain whether Fowler's stage 6 is anything other than a set of ideals towards which we reach. But to that I can refer in the final chapter.

1. E. Rayner, *Human Development* (Allen and Unwin 1978), p. 34.
2. J. W. Fowler, *Stages of Faith: the Psychology of Human Development and the Quest for Meaning* (San Francisco, Harper and Row, 1981), pp. 174–83.
3. D. W. Winnicott, *Playing and Reality* (Penguin 1974), pp. 170, 176.
4. H. Faber, *Psychology of Religion* (SCM Press 1976), p. 195.
5. ibid., pp. 285–318.
6. ibid., p. 313.
7. Fowler, *Stages of Faith*, pp. 178–9.
8. ibid., p. 178.
9. J. W. Fowler, *Becoming Adult, Becoming Christian* (San Francisco, Harper and Row, 1984) pp. 48–106; *Faith Development and Pastoral Care* (San Francisco, Harper and Row, 1987), pp. 27–51.
10. An extensive bibliography is included in A. Loades, *Searching for Lost Coins: Explorations in Christianity and Feminism* (SPCK 1987).
11. C. Gilligan, *In a Different Voice: Psychological Theory and Women's Development* (Harvard University Press 1982).
12. Faber, op. cit., pp. 275–7, where he refers to research of Godin and Hallet (1964).
13. A. Vergote, *The Religious Man* (Dublin, Gill and Macmillan, 1969).
14. D. Cupitt, *Life Lines* (SCM Press 1986).
15. W. E. Baldridge and J. J. Gleason, 'A Theological Framework for Pastoral Care' (*The Journal of Pastoral Care*, XXXII, 4, 1978), p. 235.
16. D. Lodge, *How Far Can You Go?* (Secker and Warburg 1980).
17. Fowler, *Stages of Faith*, p. 181.
18. ibid., pp. 183–98.
19. F. Page (ed.), *The Letters of John Keats* (Oxford University Press 1954), p. 86.
20. Baldridge and Gleason, op. cit., p. 235, quoting P. Tillich, *Dynamics of Faith* (New York, Harper, 1957), p. 101.

21. ibid., p. 235, quoting Tillich, op. cit., pp. 41–3.
22. Rayner. op. cit., p. 171.
23. P. W. Pruyser, *The Play of the Imagination: Towards a Psychoanalysis of Culture* (New York, International Universities Press, 1983).
24. ibid., p. 165.
25. Fowler, *Stages of Faith*, p. 198.
26. J. S. Dunne, *The Way of All the Earth: an Encounter with Eastern Religions* (Sheldon Press 1973); *The Reasons of the Heart* (SCM Press 1978); *Time and Myth* (SCM Press 1973). I am intrigued to see that Kenneth Cracknell, in his chapter on inter-faith spirituality in *Towards a New Relationship* (Epworth 1986), draws upon Keats and Dunne to illustrate his own discipline. I only discovered this after I had already used these two writers in my own development of Fowler's stage 5. This synchronicity of thought (which is not in fact attributable to any of the conversations I have had with Kenneth Cracknell, since neither of us have mentioned either author) seems to provide some confirmation of the appropriateness of this aspect of personal and faith maturity in relation to spirituality.
27. A. Samuels, *Jung and the Post-Jungians* (Routledge and Kegan Paul 1985), p. 101.
28. Fowler, *Stages of Faith*, p. 196.
29. Matt. 7:1–5.
30. M. Ford-Grabowsky, 'The Fullness of the Christian Faith Experience: Dimensions Missing in Faith Development Theory' (*The Journal of Pastoral Care* XLI, 1, 1987).
31. Fowler, *Stages of Faith*, p. 198.
32. R. L. Randall, 'Reminiscing in the Elderly: Pastoral Care of Self-Narratives' (*The Journal of Pastoral Care*, XL, 3, 1986). I refer to this at greater length in my article 'The Use of Story in Pastoral Care; Part One: Hearing Stories', in *Contact*, 1, 1988.
33. Fowler, *Stages of Faith*, p. 184.

7

Ends

Letting Go

Although it is natural to draw this enquiry into personal and Christian maturity to a close by considering ends and endings, to do so gives the impression that they are confined to the last stages of life. I have already argued that the themes that dominate growth and development cannot be restricted to one age, and this is just as true of the final theme which I now address, that of letting go. I have referred elsewhere[1] to the many 'little deaths' that accompany different stages of life, from letting go to the security of the womb to the letting go that leads to the tomb.[2] Nearly every change involves a loss as well as a potential gain. Pastoral care at the point of change provides opportunities to help people to grow through such experiences.

With the passing of years the number of occasions of losses and of letting go increases, as people experience bereavement from the death of parents and the older generation, as well as of their peers, and even of their own children. Other changes bring similar feelings, such as loss of job through redundancy and retirement, which may be accompanied by loss of social contact and of feeling useful and productive, as well as loss of financial security. Increasing age also brings with it diminution of physical fitness and agility, and greater awareness of the frailty and transience of the body. These are all factors which are to be borne in mind in pastoral care of older people, which I do not need to expand upon here. The increasing numbers and proportion of the elderly in our society requires that pastoral care addresses seriously the special needs of working with this age group.

When Erikson describes the issue of his eighth age as being

one of 'integrity versus despair', it is not difficult to imagine how the losses and changes that come with ageing might test the integrity of an old person to its limits. Fortunately years of life experience, sometimes of battling against the odds, prepare people for the adjustments that have to be made, and for many there are feelings of relief at being able to give up some of their more onerous responsibilities. Erikson includes 'renunciation' as one of the strengths of this age. Those who find it difficult to let go are more likely to be the ones who suffer if health or other circumstances compel them to do so against their will. Those who welcome the new opportunities that come with ageing and retirement have opportunities to go on growing, often engaging, unselfconsciously, in a process of integrating the memories and strands of a lifetime's experience, sufficient to withstand the potential fragmentation that so easily comes to the fore with increasing age and physical weakness.[3]

The themes of loss and of 'letting go' are important ones in many aspects of pastoral care, although I need not expand on that here, since the literature on care of the dying and the bereaved is comprehensive, including one book entitled *Letting Go*.[4] Letting go in death, as the rite of commendation recognizes, is often as much a psychological act as a physical one, with permission to let go seen in such words as: 'Go forth upon your journey from this world . . .'[5] But there are other aspects of personal letting go which are just as important to consider when reflecting upon what the fullness of Christ might mean. These aspects will not always be apparent in people because they are indications of higher points of maturity. They have their parallels in the letting go which is so much part of the final stage of life and death, inasmuch as renunciation of the self appears to be the end to which so much religious faith points. It is this which I consider first, before concluding with what appears to me to be an equally important mark of maturity, the letting go of God.

Letting Go of Self

There are considerable difficulties involved in trying to describe the final stage of Christian maturity. Those of us who make bold to do so can only be too aware that it is not a stage we have reached ourselves. It is, as Fowler says, 'extremely rare'[6] for people to reach his stage 6, that of Universalizing Faith. It is a stage which can only be described through paradox, although Fowler appears to experience more difficulty introducing his stage 5 (Conjunctive Faith), than he does his stage 6. Any attempt to understand both the final stages depends less upon intellectual comprehension, and more upon 'seeing' as in the term 'insight'. Words do not fail completely, but they only make sense when a person has had the same experience. Fingarette, upon whose work I draw considerably in this section, observes that the problem of describing experience is as real for the psychoanalytic patient as it is for the mystic, since it 'involves a peculiar shifting of mental gears'.[7] Insight, or the mystic vision, cannot arise out of a conscious act of will; we cannot make ourselves experience 'Aha!' moments; they come, to use the language of metaphor, 'out of the blue'. Even when such moments have come, and gone, we are often left as much in the dark as before, although we know we have caught a glimpse of something. It is like being out on a dark night, when a flash of lightning unforgettably and briefly lights up our surroundings, but leaves us as quickly as it came: and no better able to physically see our way forward than before, even though we are left with a mental impression that guides our path.

Fowler makes difficulties by suggesting a radical difference between Conjunctive and Universalizing Faith, which puts the final stage effectively out of reach, except for the very few. As I indicated in the last chapter, Fowler says that Conjunctive Faith involves a much broader vision of symbol and myth, yet carries the risk with it of paralyzing inaction, as people in this stage find themselves caught between the vision and the reality. There may well be a vision of a fairer world, of the common joys and sorrows that unite the peoples of the world, but stage 5, even when such visions are translated into activity, is one which remains, according to Fowler, paradoxical and divided, 'because the self is caught between universalizing apprehensions and the need to preserve its own being and well-being'.[8]

What distinguishes stage 6 most from stage 5, he says, is that it involves a shift of concern. Threats to the self cease to deter a person from speaking out. The primary group of which he or she is a member, or the institutions of the present order, are only vehicles to help achieve his or her vision, and are equally open to change. Persons of this stage are less concerned with self-preservation; they exhibit more transcendent moral and religious qualities; they have a vision of a universal community, and they often invoke non-violent strategies to achieve their vision. He lists as examples of such people Gandhi, Martin Luther King, Mother Teresa of Calcutta (the only woman included), Bonhoeffer and Thomas Merton, although he concedes that he cannot simply list the renowned and that there must be many others. But if there are many others, then this stage is no longer 'exceedingly rare'. In another book[9] he lists this stage as part of middle adulthood and beyond (as if it were normal) and yet omits it from his exploration of types of congregational presence – as if it is never found in congregations as a whole. Yet if those he has listed are to achieve their vision, they need others who share and carry it through, followers who are equally prepared to renounce their own lives for the sake of the vision. Many of the great revolutionaries (in religion or politics) have succeeded not on their own, but because they were the representative of a body of people who shared the same ideals and principles.

Fowler tends to idealize when he comes to describe Universalizing Faith, in order to make it 'special'. His description[10] of stage 6 people oozes with unctuousness. He talks, for instance, of their 'redemptive subversiveness' and their 'relevant irrelevance', as though the language of paradox had gone to his head. He mentions that many of those in this stage die at the hands of those whom they hope to change; this is because while they liberate, they also threaten. They show up (though not intentionally) the inconsistencies which exist in the rest of us. 'They are more lucid, more simple, and yet somehow more fully human than the rest of us.' They love life, but hold on to it loosely. They are ready for fellowship with people at any of the other stages and from any other faith tradition. The communities[11] they seek to foster are inclusive of others too. Usefully, and necessarily, Fowler distinguishes between stage 6 people and fanatics, who likewise often have a vision, and often carry with them a religious community that wishes to unite the world. They too demonstrate their willingness to die for the cause; but the fanatic, and the fanatical community, seeks unity and the fulfilment of vision on the basis of forcing others to conform, and not on the basis of freedom and love.[12]

The difficulties of comprehending stage 6 (except by reference to a list of 'saints', such as Fowler appears to 'canonize') can be eased by dropping the stage altogether, except as a description of the true direction in which stage 5 people are moving or, like Kohlberg's 'stage 7', as a metaphor or an ideal state. Stage 6, if it is separate at all, helps us describe peaks of insight, and action based upon experience. But I doubt whether anyone can be placed as permanently in such a stage. Merton's official biographer,[13] for instance, makes clear a number of examples of self-centredness even when he had attracted a huge and devoted following for his vision of the contemplative life, of world peace and of inter-faith understanding. Erikson was very critical of certain of Gandhi's characteristics. Fowler qualifies his description of stage 6 people by saying that they are neither perfect, nor fully 'actualized' (to use Maslow's term), and that they have their limitations. In answer to others' criticism of the lack of any clear difference between stage 5 and stage 6 types of faith, Fowler argues that stage 6 people are distinguished by the 'breakthrough of Spirit'; that up to the fifth stage we see 'natural' development, but achievement of stage 6 is through 'grace'.[14] This limiting and limited idea of grace is not one which many people will find satisfactory.

These problems are removed by adopting a more simple approach, which straightforwardly integrates the main features of Universalizing Faith (stage 6) with Conjunctive Faith (stage 5). Stage 5 then allows for a continuum, from the recognition that other people have viewpoints which inform our own thinking, to a more universal appreciation of faith, including that of other religions as well as our own. It permits the renunciation of the self, ranging from letting go of self-concern to preparedness to lose one's life for the sake of what is true. Stage 5 then includes the 'aha' experiences which many people know, as well as those moments of sublime vision when 'the whole world is charged with the grandeur of God'.[15] Stage 5 may give rise to the type of paralysis of action that comes from difficulty in coming to terms with the paradoxical vision described earlier, or to the type of self-sacrificing action that may result in having to give up one's life; or at least aspects of one's life. However for most stage 5 people, there is probably a blend of thought and action which lies somewhere between inactivity on the one hand and martyrdom on the other. Stage 6, if it is of any value at all, is as a reminder of the potentiality for maturity, and of the deepest expression of faith. We may catch glimpses of both, but cannot hang on to, or stay with, either.

Nevertheless, Fowler's concentration on lack of self-concern as being one of the marks of maturity, first appearing in stage 5, is very valuable, as long as it does not expect martyrdom to be its normal outcome! It provides a fascinating link with more general psychological maturity, which, like perfect faith, can never be achieved, although it can be spoken about as an ideal. Fingarette observes that there can never be a state of being 'fully analyzed', but that psychoanalysis can also speak of what this would mean as a goal worth aiming at.[16]

Fingarette compares the outcome of successful psychoanalysis with the height of mystical experience. One feature that they both have in common is that analysand and mystic cease to be so self-conscious. Most of us are, to different degrees, 'compulsive, obsessive, acutely self-conscious, focusing . . . attention upon our feelings and our perceptions, our theoretical distinctions and logical proofs.'[17] Letting go of self, Fingarette suggests, does not involve self-negation as such, but being able to let go of this type of self-consciousness. It is this which is involved in the way of enlightenment (he draws more heavily upon Eastern than upon Western mysticism to illustrate his argument). But enlightenment does not mean the loss of 'sensing, perceiving, thinking, discriminating [which] are essential functions within the enlightened life'. These four qualities are very similar to the four personality types proposed by Jung. In Jungian theory, maturation and individuation includes integration of the thinking, feeling, intuitive and sensing parts of the personality, which 'merge so that a person's conscious attitudes, and hence a greater part of his experience of himself, will become richer and more variegated.'[18]

Fingarette illustrates how a person who has experienced the benefits of psychoanalysis to the full also shows the characteristic of the mystic – a sense of 'not being concerned' about the self. For example, such a person does not feel angry for her or himself, or does not easily get upset if other people say things that are intended to hurt. The person enjoys life, but is not dependent upon it. The self has been sufficiently integrated for it to be let go of, and for it not to matter what other people think or say. This does not imply that analysis, any more than mystic experience, leads to a person being withdrawn, or cool, as if they 'couldn't care less'. There is in both the mystic and the analysed person intense participation, warmth, and ability to feel, but without self-concern. He recognizes, of course, that no one is fully analyzed, just as no one is completely enlightened.[19]

Terms such as integration and integrity, individuation and maturity thus have some features in common with the way mystical writers describe the fruition of spirituality. Without having to resort, as Fowler does, to lists of 'saints', Fingarette helps us to understand from our own more limited experience, or our own less than complete analysis, that the gradual freeing of a person from self-concern is different from a self that is to be denied or negated, as a cursory reading of spiritual writing might have us believe. Guntrip expressed this relationship between self and self-giving well when he wrote: 'The peak of maturity . . . [is] to be able to give oneself to the utmost in love, for convincing reasons, without loss of ego-integrity.'[20] Personal growth, particularly in these later stages of development, leads to lessening of the three basic types of anxiety found in Tillich's analysis.[21] The move away from the secondary narcissism of young adulthood (and of Fowler's stage 4) is helped by the growing realization in the second half of life of the inevitability of death, leading, for those who move into Conjunctive Faith, to less anxiety about fate or death. Here too, in stage 5, where the search for meaning is enriched by the wisdom of one's own and of other faiths, a person begins to replenish the vacuum of emptiness and loss of meaning, which earlier conventional beliefs might have failed to satisfy. Finally, the deeper self-analysis (perhaps with the help of the pastor or therapist), which is part of the movement towards individuation and integrity, helps edge a person away from the sterile preoccupation with guilt and condemnation, to deeper self-knowledge and self-confidence. This leads, again in Tillich's terms, to the courage to be oneself, the courage to be a full participant in the community and in the world, and – taking us into my concluding pages – the courage to be rooted in 'the God above God'.[22]

Letting Go of God

The traditional religious view is to see union with God as the pinnacle of experience and therefore of spiritual maturity. It is more than simply growing separateness and selfhood, even if that selfhood involves concern for others and the absence of self-consciousness that I have described above. Unity with the divine, in mystical experience and in more down-to-earth spirituality, is not simply seen as a future promise after death, but as a possibility in the present. But what does union with God mean?

Freud thought that the desire for spiritual bliss was a wish for the return of the oceanic feelings of childhood, originally experienced in the symbiotic mother–baby relationship. Both he and Jung, however, are criticized by Wilbur, a transpersonal psychologist: Freud, for reducing the transcendent to the prepersonal; and Jung, for elevating everything from the prepersonal to the transcendent. It would be confusing to introduce at this late point yet another model of development, so I pass over the first four stages proposed by Wilbur,[23] because they show considerable overlap with various models which I have already outlined in preceding chapters. What is more important is to observe the particular emphasis which transpersonal psychology gives to the dynamic relationship between the personal (the first four stages in Wilbur and in Fowler) and the transpersonal, which Wilbur describes as 'the Ultimate', 'the Spirit', 'the Transcendent' and 'God'. Wilbur, like some of Fowler's critics, argues the need to transcend ego-psychology and to grow into harmony with the transcendent Being of the Universe. So the fifth stage in

Wilbur's model has similarities to Fowler's stage 5, since it moves beyond the ego to a more 'panoramic' vision, towards deep integrity, towards archetypes (Jung's term), towards transcendent awareness, and towards the source and ground of all structures. Wilbur's sixth stage is that of 'Spirit', 'pure Being' and 'God', and links in with the substance of this final chapter.

What is particularly pertinent to this study is Wilbur's assertion that union with the transcendent is not the same as the primary oneness of infancy. The state of the infant is one of ignorance, so that he cannot yet be one with the world, whether it is the personal world or the symbolic world. We must not confuse the all-embracing microcosm of the infant with the vastness of the universe as we begin to realize it in adult life.[24] Fingarette agrees, quoting Meister Eckhart with approval: 'One must achieve this unself-consciousness by means of transformed knowledge. *This* ignorance does not come from lack of self-knowledge but rather it is from knowledge that one may achieve this ignorance.'[25] Fingarette distinguishes between the naivety of a child, and the humility of the person who has learned from life experience. This distinction is important, and relevant to the theme of letting go, because there is clearly in many respects a similarity between the transcendent feelings that come with the stages of Conjunctive and Universalizing Faith, and the 'blooming buzzing confusion' of stage 0, Primal Faith. A similar link between first and last stages is made by Erikson when he writes that 'where adults have integrity enough not to fear death, their children will not fear life'.[26] Yet the wisdom which Erikson associates with old age, comes about partly through the second virtue which he includes in that period of life – renunciation, the ability to let go, including at times the letting go of more certain ways of knowing (particularly the rational).

Yet a unified vision of the transcendent cannot simply be gained by seeking after it. Such experience breaks in from outside, just as Christians believe to be the case in the action of the Holy Spirit, whom it is possible to describe as both passively indwelling, but also as actively 'leading'. Fingarette equates psychoanalytic insight with mystic experience as being passively received (from a person's own consciousness) rather than actively produced.[27] It is not something that can be deliberately searched for. The Christian mystics warn against the seduction of seeking trances and visions. Perhaps the most apt religious imagery for such experience is the hound of heaven imagery,[28] reminding us that the transcendent breaks through at the point we cease chasing not only away from, but also chasing after the transcendent.

Unlike Wilbur, Fingarette prefers to view the loss of self in unity with God – or the One in Eastern mysticism – as a definite regression to childhood. He believes that it is an experience of natural creative regression, just as going back to infancy is part of therapy itself.[29] The psychoanalytic belief in the self-regulation of the ego requires a person to go back to beginnings in order to develop. There is therefore every justification for the mystic, who reaches to the heights of maturity, like the mythical 'fully analyzed patient', to regress more in order to develop more.

He reminds us, however, that 'union with God or dwelling in God' is not 'union with a substantial person, or existence in a definite place'.[30] That is a naive (mis)representation of what mystics say. For this reason I want to question Fowler's suggestion (even though it is qualified) that the culmination of stage 6 Universalizing Faith is to be seen in the radical monotheism of the Judaeo-Christian tradition.[31] I have the same concern about such a statement as I do about his choice of stage 6 individuals, because I think he is choosing his own religious tradition simply because he holds it dear, and needs to elevate it to this status. But which form of Judaeo-Christian radical monotheism would Fowler isolate as the culmination? In a psychoanalytic study of religion, Badcock[32] accords a high place to Renaissance Catholicism, although he takes psychoanalysis itself as the culmination of culture. Clearly, we tend to accord the highest place to that which we hold most valuable and true.

Fowler also appears to contradict his elevation of Judaeo-Christian monotheism when he describes the last two stages of development, Conjunctive and Universalizing Faith as inclusive, learning from other traditions. This steers us away (appropriately) from slavish dependency upon our own faith to the sentiments of W. H. Auden's phrase, 'All poets . . . are polytheists,' where the imagination is capable of embracing 'all kinds of other ideas and aspirations and hopes, things that are to be loved and worshipped'.[33] In the highest reaches of maturity all but the language of poetry and metaphor fails us; but even then at one and the same time poetic language both enriches and limits our understanding.

Perhaps, as Jones[34] suggests, there is a stage of maturity beyond the imagery of Ignatian spirituality and Jungian individuation, or the language of poetry. He believes that Jung in particular needs the *via negativa* to 'slow him down'. Jones would have us go beyond Jung to Freud and to the point at which, in chapter 4, I began looking at human and faith development. Transference analysis, which includes analysis of the language we use about God, is akin to the desert fathers, who knew transference in some of the images and visions they experienced. Jones sees certain patterns in common between psychoanalysis and the *via negativa* of the desert fathers, such as: the need for detachment; the belief that nothing is accidental; the assertion that we are not as free as we like to think we are; the value of remembering as an important part of growth (which of course especially applies to the last stage of life when remembering features so strongly); the conviction that while much of what we do has to be done alone, companionship is essential; the necessity for contemplative commitment; an appreciation of our fallenness; and, especially pertinent at this point, the mystery of having to let go of the things and the people we love the most. Clearly this also means all our language, and even our thinking about God.

Whether therefore it is Tillich's 'God above God', or Bonhoeffer's 'religionless Christianity', or Freud's reduction of language about God to the status of transference projections, we find much in common between the theological and the psychological approach to maturity. These aspects of theology and psychology are also supported by the *via negativa* as one way of spirituality. It is an important, if neglected, part of the mystical tradition, in which all language about God is in the negative: God is *not* this and *not* that, even as in the mystic 'Dionysius the Areopagite' God is not God.

Leech, in his extensive survey of spiritual theology, only makes one reference to the *via negativa*,[35] although it is an important one. He writes that authentic mysticism involves 'a confrontation with all forms of illusion and pretence within our own persons and in our society. The mystical way is essentially subversive ... the *via negativa* has profound political implications'. The subversive nature of true mysticism accords with Fowler's description of stage 6 persons as 'subversive of the structures (including religious structures) by which we sustain our corporate survival, security and significance'.[36]

The illusion which Leech refers to has to include the illusion about religion, of which Freud provided clinical evidence and explanation.[37] A Freudian view of religion perhaps urges a pure form of faith, free from illusion, consonant with the highest points of religious thought.

> The end of religion ... is God. Contrariwise, God is the end of religion in the sense that once He appears vividly before us, in His depth and love and unrelenting truth, all else dissolves, or at the least religious paraphernalia drop back into their due and mundane place, and the concept 'religion' is brought to an end.[38]

These words of Cantwell Smith's will, I am sure, be interpreted in as many ways as there are readers of them. For some the end of religion will be their vision of God as personal, because their imagination can grasp no other. For me, when I am able to think at a high level of abstraction (which is difficult to sustain for long, because I, like others, also prefer the security and colour of images) the end of religion means that all our language, all our symbols, all our churches, all our doctrines and creeds actually disappear before the immensity of the concept of the transcendent:

> Right views are called 'transcendental',
> Erroneous views are called 'worldly',
> But when all views, both right and erroneous, are
>   discarded.
> Then the essence of Wisdom manifests itself.[39]

This bears out the coupling of wisdom with renunciation,

which as I have already indicated Erikson describes as the two virtues most appropriate to the last age of mature adulthood. And if this is a strange note upon which to finish a book which, like all writing, uses the medium of words, metaphor, and concrete ideas, it is not, of course, to deny the importance of good pastoral care through all the preceding stages of development, where signs and symbols in various ways speak for and to us. To finish on this note of letting go of all imagery, language and symbol, in other words, letting go of God,[40] is rather to urge that, as a church, we have a very long way to go on the path towards the kind of maturity, which in its very *kenosis* (emptying) contains the fullness of Christ. 'For our knowledge and our prophecy alike are partial, and the partial vanishes when wholeness comes.'[41]

1. M. Jacobs, *Still Small Voice* (SPCK 1982), pp. 143–5.
2. See the anecdote in J. W. Fowler, *Becoming Adult, Becoming Christian* (San Francisco, Harper and Row, 1984), p. 30. Fowler refers to epigrams invented by Erikson's students to describe the life cycle: 'from womb to tomb, from bust to dust, etc.'
3. I gather, although I cannot cite any reference to check this, that Winnicott, although he was not himself a conventionally religious man, wrote the following at the start of a journal he kept when he knew he was going to die from a lung disease: 'Prayer: O God, may I be alive when I die.'
4. P. Speck, and I. Ainsworth-Smith, *Letting Go: Caring for the Dying and Bereaved* (SPCK 1982).
5. Ministry to the Sick (*Authorized Alternative Services*) (SPCK 1983), p. 37.
6. J. W. Fowler, *Stages of Faith: the Psychology of Human Development and the Quest for Meaning* (San Francisco, Harper and Row, 1981), p. 200.
7. H. Fingarette, *The Self in Transformation* (New York, Basic Books, 1963), pp. 327–30.
8. Fowler, *Stages of Faith*, p. 200.
9. J. W. Fowler, *Faith Development and Pastoral Care* (Fortress Press 1987).
10. Fowler, *Stages of Faith*, pp. 200–1.
11. Notice in his 1981 book (ibid.) Fowler includes communities of stage 6 faith (p. 201), even though he omits them in his 1987 book.

12. Nevertheless, Islamic fundamentalists might also think in terms of freedom and love, with different (more violent) means to the same end. Clearly there are questions raised here by such a distinction, which require the help of moral philosophy for answers.
13. M. Mott, *The Seven Mountains of Thomas Merton* (Sheldon Press 1986).
14. Fowler, *Becoming Adult, Becoming Christian*, pp. 72–4.
15. Gerard Manley Hopkins: 'God's Grandeur', in *Gerard Manley Hopkins: a Selection of his Poems and Prose*, ed. W. H. Gardner, (Penguin 1953).
16. Fingarette. op. cit., p. 335.
17. ibid., p. 319.
18. A. Samuels, *Jung and the Post-Jungians* (Routledge and Kegan Paul 1985), pp. 62–4.
19. Figarette. op. cit., p. 295.
20. H. Guntrip, *Psychoanalytic Theory, Therapy and the Self* (Hogarth Press 1971), p. 124.
21. P. Tillich, *The Courage to Be* (Nisbet 1952), pp. 37–51.
22. ibid., pp. 176–80.
23. For a summary of Wilbur's theory, see W. S. Schmidt, 'An Ontological Model of Development' (*The Journal of Pastoral Care*, xxxx, 1, 1986, pp. 56–67). He cites various writings of Wilbur's, including K. Wilbur, *Up from Eden: a Transpersonal View of Human Evolution* (New York, Anchor Press/Doubleday, 1981).
24. Schmidt, op. cit., p. 58.
25. Fingarette, op. cit., p. 324.
26. E. Erikson, *Childhood and Society* (Penguin 1965), p. 261.
27. Fingarette, op. cit., p. 329.
28. Psalm 139:7, although the whole psalm expresses much that is relevant here, including the imagery of the womb and of infancy.
29. Fingarette, op. cit., pp. 332–4.
30. ibid., p. 336.
31. Fowler, *Stages of Faith*, pp. 204–11.
32. C. R. Badcock, *The Psychoanalysis of Culture* (Oxford, Blackwell, 1980), p. 253.
33. K. Cracknell, *Towards a New Relationship* (Epworth 1986), p. 143, where the reference to Auden also appears.
34. A. Jones, *Soul Making* (SCM Press 1986).
35. K. Leech, *True God* (Sheldon Press 1985), p. 348.
36. Fowler, *Stages of Faith*, p. 201.
37. S. Freud, 'A Question of a Weltanschauung' in *New Introductory*

Lectures on Psychoanalysis, Pelican Freud Library; vol. 2 (Penguin 1973), ch. 35.

38. W. Cantwell Smith, *The Meaning and End of Religion* (SPCK 1978), p. 201, quoted by Cracknell (op. cit., p. 191).
39. Fingarette, op. cit., p. 323. These lines are a quotation from a Buddhist source.
40. 'I pray God to rid me of God. The highest and loftiest thing that one can let go of is to let go of God for the sake of God.' I was shown this quotation after writing this chapter, and was pleased to find that Meister Eckhart had been there before me! The quotation appears in M. Fox, *Meditations with Eckhart* (Santa Fé, Bear and Co., 1983), p. 50.
41. 1 Cor. 13:9 (NEB).

Bibliography

Badcock, C. R., *The Psychoanalysis of Culture*. Oxford, Blackwell, 1980.

Baldridge, W. E. and Gleason, J. J., 'A Theological Framework for Pastoral Care', *The Journal of Pastoral Care*, XXXII, 4, 1978.

Belotti, E., *Little Girls*. London, Readers and Writers Co-operative, 1985.

Bryant, C., *The Heart in Pilgrimage*. Darton Longman and Todd 1980.

Campbell, A. V., *Rediscovering Pastoral Care*. Darton Longman and Todd, rev. edn 1986.

Cantwell Smith, W., *Faith and Belief*. Princeton University Press 1979.

Cantwell Smith, W., *The Meaning and End of Religion*. SPCK 1978.

Capps, D., *Life Cycle Theory and Pastoral Care*. Fortress Press 1983.

Capps, D., *Pastoral Care: a Thematic Approach*. Philadelphia, Westminster Press, 1969.

Carr, W., *Brief Encounters*. SPCK 1985.

Chodorow, N., *The Reproduction of Mothering*. University of California Press 1978.

Colledge, E., and Walsh, J. (trans.), *Julian of Norwich: Showings*. Paulist Press and SPCK 1978.

Cracknell, K., *Towards a New Relationship*. Epworth Press 1986.

Cupitt, D., *Life Lines*. SCM Press 1986.

Dunne, J. S., *The Reasons of the Heart*. SCM Press 1978.

Dunne, J. S., *Time and Myth*. SCM Press 1973.

Dunne, J. S., *The Way of All the Earth: an Encounter with Eastern Religions*. Sheldon Press 1973.

Eliot, T. S., 'Burnt Norton' in *Four Quartets*. Faber 1959.

Erikson, E., *Childhood and Society*. Penguin 1965.

Erikson, E., *Gandhi's Truth*. New York, W. W. Norton, 1969.

Erikson, E., *Young Man Luther*. Faber 1959.

Faber, H., *Psychology of Religion*. SCM Press 1976.

Fingarette, H., *The Self in Transformation.* New York, Basic Books, 1963.
Ford-Grabowsky, M., 'The Fullness of the Christian Faith Experience: Dimensions Missing in Faith Development Theory', *The Journal of Pastoral Care*, XLI, 1, 1987.
Fordham, Frieda, *An Introduction to Jung's Psychology.* Penguin 1966.
Fowler, J. W., *Becoming Adult, Becoming Christian.* San Francisco, Harper and Row, 1984.
Fowler, J. W., *Faith Development and Pastoral Care.* Fortress Press 1987.
Fowler, J. W., *Stages of Faith: the Psychology of Human Development and the Quest for Meaning.* San Francisco, Harper and Row, 1981.
Fox, M., *Meditations with Eckhart.* Santa Fé, Bear and Co., 1983.
Freud, A., *Normality and Pathology in Childhood.* Penguin 1973.
Freud, S., *New Introductory Lectures on Psychoanalysis*, Freud Library, vol. 2, Penguin 1973.
Freud, S., *Obsessive Actions and Religious Practices*, Freud Library, vol. 13. Penguin 1985.
Fromm, E., *Psychoanalysis and Religion.* Yale University Press 1967.
Gardner, W. H., *Gerard Manley Hopkins: a Selection of his Poems and Prose.* Penguin 1953.
Gatta, J., *A Pastoral Art.* Darton Longman and Todd 1987.
Gilligan, C., *In a Different Voice: Psychological Theory and Women's Development.* Harvard University Press 1982.
Golan, Naomi, *Passing Through Transitions.* London, Collier Macmillan, 1981.
Goldman, R., *Readiness for Religion.* Routledge and Kegan Paul 1965.
Goldman, R., *Religious Thinking from Childhood to Adolescence.* Routledge and Kegan Paul 1964.
Guntrip, H., *Psychoanalytic Theory, Therapy and the Self.* Hogarth Press 1971.
Harding, D. E., *On Having No Head.* London and New York, Arkana, 1986.
Hemenway, Joan, 'Four Faith Frameworks', *The Journal of Pastoral Care*, XXXVIII, 4, 1984.
Hughes, G., *The God of Surprises.* Darton Longman and Todd 1985.
Jacobs, M. (ed.), *Faith or Fear.* Darton Longman and Todd 1987.
Jacobs, M., 'Naming and Labelling', *Contact*, 3, 1976.
Jacobs, M., *The Presenting Past.* Open University Press 1986.
Jacobs, M., *Still Small Voice*, SPCK 1982.
Jacobs, M., 'The Use of Story in Pastoral Care. Part One: Hearing Stories', *Contact*, 1, 1988.
Jones, A., *Soul Making.* SCM Press 1986.

Justice, W. G. and Lambert, W., 'A Comparative Study of the Language People Use to Describe the Personalities of God and their Earthly Parents', *The Journal of Pastoral Care*, XL, 2, 1986.

Kohlberg, L., 'Education, Moral Development and Faith', *Journal of Moral Education*, IV, 1.

Kohlberg, L., *The Philosophy of Moral Development*. San Francisco, Harper and Row, 1981.

Leech, K., *True God*. Sheldon Press 1985.

Levinson, D. *et al.*, *The Seasons of a Man's Life*. New York, Knopf, 1978.

Lewis, C. S., *The Last Battle*. Penguin 1964.

Loades, A., *Searching for Lost Coins: Explorations in Christianity and Feminism*. SPCK 1987.

Lodge, D., *How Far Can You Go?* Secker and Warburg 1980.

McFague, Sallie, *Models of God*. Fortress Press and SCM Press, 1987.

Ministry to the Sick *(Authorized Alternative Services)*. SPCK 1983.

Mott, M., *The Seven Mountains of Thomas Merton*. Sheldon Press 1986.

Page, F. (ed), *The Letters of John Keats*. Oxford University Press 1954.

Philips, J. L., *The Origins of Intellect*. USA, W. H. Freeman, 1975.

Pruyser, P. W., *The Play of the Imagination: Towards a Psychoanalysis of Culture*. New York, International Universities Press, 1983.

Randall, R. L., 'Reminiscing in the Elderly: Pastoral Care of Self-Narratives', *The Journal of Pastoral Care*, XL, 3, 1986.

Randall, R. L. 'Stages in the Role Cycle of Pastoral Counseling', *The Journal of Pastoral Care*, XXXVI, 2, 1982.

Rayner, E., *Human Development*. Allen and Unwin 1978.

Reed, B., *The Dynamics of Religion*. Darton Longman and Todd 1978.

Renner, H. P. V., 'The Use of Ritual in Pastoral Care', *The Journal of Pastoral Care*, XXXIII, 3, 1979.

Rizzuto, Anna-Maria, *The Birth of the Living God*, University of Chicago Press 1979.

Rogers, C., *Freedom to Learn*. Ohio, Merrill, 1969.

Samuels, A., *Jung and the Post-Jungians*. Routledge and Kegan Paul 1985.

Schlauch, C. R., 'Defining Pastoral Psychotherapy', *The Journal of Pastoral Care*, XXXIX, 3, 1985.

Schmidt, W. S., 'An Ontological Model of Development', *The Journal of Pastoral Care*, XL, 1, 1986.

Speck, P. and Ainsworth-Smith, I., *Letting Go: Caring for the Dying and Bereaved*. SPCK 1982.

Tillich, P., *The Courage to Be*. Nisbet 1952.

Tillich, P. *Dynamics of Faith*. New York, Harper, 1957.

Vergote, A., *The Religious Man*. Dublin, Gill and Macmillan, 1969.
Wilbur, K., *Up from Eden: a Transpersonal View of Human Evolution*. New York, Anchor Press/Doubleday, 1981.
Winnicott, D. W., *Home is Where We Start From*. Penguin 1986.
Winnicott, D. W., *The Maturational Processes and the Facilitating Environment*. Tavistock Publications 1965.
Winnicott, D. W., *Playing and Reality*. Penguin 1974.
Winnicott, D. W., 'Transitional Objects and Transitional Phenomena', *Collected Papers*. Tavistock Publications 1958.

Index